Philosophical, Educational, and Moral Openings in Doctoral Pursuits and Supervision

This timely volume conceptualises and applies the philosophical notions of wonder, wander, and whisper, serving as evaluative paradigms for objective assessment of quality doctoral research work and supervision in South African higher education.

Written by one of the foremost academics in the field, the book combines the normative philosophical, educational, and moral notions of wonder, wander, and whisper with academic life and studies, focusing on doctoral work and supervision not just as cognitive or scientific processes, but also as existential, ethical, and political shaping of the self. By reflecting on three decades of doctoral supervision, the author gives an account of how his students have been initiated into moral discourses of democratic citizenship education and the intellectual adventures they have embarked upon through scholarly texts. The book also presents itself as a decolonial venture that repositions and resituates doctoral education in resistance to the hegemony of colonisation, inhumanity, inequality, unfreedom, and injustice in Southern Africa.

Ultimately arguing for the relevance of wonder, wander, and whisper in academic culture, the book will appeal to scholars, researchers, and postgraduates in the fields of higher education, philosophy of education, and sociology of education, as well as African education and doctoral studies more broadly.

Yusef Waghid is Distinguished Professor of Philosophy of Education, Stellenbosch University, South Africa.

Routledge Research in Higher Education

Creating Supportive Spaces for Pregnant and Parenting College Students
Contemporary Understandings of Title IX
Edited by Catherine L. Riley and Katie B. Garner

Gamification and Design Thinking in Higher Education
Case Studies for Instructional Innovation in the Economics Classroom
Carmen Bueno Muñoz, Núria Hernández Nanclares, Luis R. Murillo Zamorano, and José Ángel López Sánchez

The Development of Professional Identity in Higher Education
Continuing and Advancing Professionalism
Edited by Myint Swe Khine and Abdulghani Muthanna

Internships, High-Impact Practices, and Provocative Praxis in Higher Education
A Social Justice Framework Based on Equity, Diversity, Inclusion, and Access
Beth Manke, Bonnie Gasior, and Michelle Chang

Philosophical, Educational, and Moral Openings in Doctoral Pursuits and Supervision
Promoting the Values of Wonder, Wander, and Whisper in African Higher Education
Yusef Waghid

For more information about this series, please visit: www.routledge.com/Routledge-Research-in-Higher-Education/book-series/RRHE

Philosophical, Educational, and Moral Openings in Doctoral Pursuits and Supervision
Promoting the Values of Wonder, Wander, and Whisper in African Higher Education

Yusef Waghid

LONDON AND NEW YORK

First published 2024
by Routledge
4 Park Square, Milton Park, Abingdon, Oxon OX14 4RN

and by Routledge
605 Third Avenue, New York, NY 10158

Routledge is an imprint of the Taylor & Francis Group, an informa business

© 2024 Yusef Waghid

The right of Yusef Waghid to be identified as author of this work has been asserted in accordance with sections 77 and 78 of the Copyright, Designs and Patents Act 1988.

All rights reserved. No part of this book may be reprinted or reproduced or utilised in any form or by any electronic, mechanical, or other means, now known or hereafter invented, including photocopying and recording, or in any information storage or retrieval system, without permission in writing from the publishers.

Trademark notice: Product or corporate names may be trademarks or registered trademarks, and are used only for identification and explanation without intent to infringe.

British Library Cataloguing-in-Publication Data
A catalogue record for this book is available from the British Library

Library of Congress Cataloging-in-Publication Data
Names: Waghid, Yusef, author.
Title: Philosophical, educational, and moral openings in doctoral pursuits and supervision : promoting the values of wonder, wander, and whisper in African higher education / Yusef Waghid. Other titles: Routledge research in higher education.
Description: New York : Routledge, 2024. | Series: Routledge research in higher education | Includes bibliographical references and index.
Identifiers: LCCN 2023047657 (print) | LCCN 2023047658 (ebook) | ISBN 9781032713731 (hardback) | ISBN 9781032715643 (paperback) | ISBN 9781032715872 (ebook)
Subjects: LCSH: Doctoral students—Supervision of—Africa—Philosophy. | Universities and colleges—Africa—Graduate work—Philosophy. | Dissertations, Academic—Research—Africa—Philosophy. | Wonder. | Decolonization—Africa.
Classification: LCC LB2386 W344 2024 (print) | LCC LB2386 (ebook) | DDC 378.1794096—dc23
LC record available at https://lccn.loc.gov/2023047657
LC ebook record available at https://lccn.loc.gov/2023047658

ISBN: 978-1-032-71373-1 (hbk)
ISBN: 978-1-032-71564-3 (pbk)
ISBN: 978-1-032-71587-2 (ebk)

DOI: 10.4324/9781032715872

Typeset in Times New Roman
by Apex CoVantage, LLC

Contents

	Preface	vii
1	University education and the quest to wonder	1
2	Wandering and university education: in pursuit of poiesis, praxis, and rhythm	9
3	Whispering as studious and playful university education	14
4	On utopianism and doctoral education	20
5	Towards ethical pedagogical encounters between supervisors and students	26
6	Doctoral supervision and the enactment of democratic citizenship education	32
7	Doctoral education and the enactment of cosmopolitan justice	38
8	Doctoral supervision and the notion of critique	43
9	Doctoral education as profanation and play	47
10	A personal narrative on doctoral adventures	51
11	On questioning reasoned and democratic universities: towards an *ubuntu* university	59

12 On autonomous, iterative, and restorative doctoral
   supervision: a glimpse into the future   65

13 On decolonised doctoral education   70

   Afterword: A personal reflection on conditioned thought   76
   Index   93

Preface

Introduction

Nowadays, university education in South Africa seems to be in a quandary: the waning of critical reason, academic posturing, democratic illusions, a dearth of genuine scholars, and the presence of corrupt practices at some higher education institutions, all contribute to a culture of lameness in our universities. Put differently, higher education in Southern Africa seems to endure some kind of moral dilemma. My use of morality in this book involves recognising that something is wrong in higher education discourse. On the basis of my engagement with thoughts in and about doctoral education, I offer a way to rectify a dilemma in higher education. In the latter regard, I offer a return to an authentic university in terms of wondering, wandering, and whispering to counteract a limping university focusing on doctoral education and supervision.

A university loses its capacity for critical reasoning if it no longer serves the purpose of an institution that uses and relies extensively on argumentation and debate to enhance its existence. When academic pursuits (like doctoral education) are no longer advanced in the interest of critical reason, a university fails to uphold its esteemed intellectual and moral position in society. I am specifically referring to some established universities in Southern Africa confronted by corrupt practices such as conferring (doctoral) degrees on some students undeserved of such an accolade. So what causes a university to lose its critical reason? Such a university subverts knowledge production and assigns the quest for knowledge and its advancement to the abyss of mere technicist claims – that knowledge ought to be produced to serve the utilitarian demands of the economy, politics, and bureaucracy. Long gone would be the goal of advancing knowledge for its own sake, considered by me as a moral dilemma. Invariably, academics are required to serve as technicians whose function merely provides a recipe for societal change, such as producing new devices for communication, identification, and innovation. The arguments in this book examine the purposes of knowledge differently, more specifically, away from the technicist demands of producing external paraphernalia but rather why universities, in the first place, should remain institutions of knowledge (re)construction and deconstruction. I have decided to focus on doctoral education and supervision for such an examination.

At the centre of my intellectual activities – that is, my engagement and knowledge claims – is a resistance towards a form of higher education that advances what has come to be known as exclusive colonial knowledge. What is wrong with colonial knowledge? Under the guise of modernisation, colonial knowledge is meant to enslave and rationally exploit people (Young, 2005). Through colonial knowledge, power is dispensed to directly appropriate and exploit the resources and labour of marginalised peoples (McClintock, 1994). In the main, colonial knowledge is meant to dominate people, deterritorialise people, and exploit already marginalised peoples through violence, torture, and other means of suppression (Harris, 2004). Before 1994, South African higher education was subjected to colonial knowledge patterns that excluded most of the marginalised population. Today, some remnants of colonial knowledge claims remain prevalent in some university curricula that undermine the legitimate participation of many students in the curriculum processes. The presence of colonial knowledge excludes many marginalised students from authentic participation in university curricula. Hence, these students remain excluded (Waghid et al., 2023). The dilemma of colonised knowledge claims, I argue throughout this book, should be resisted and be rethought along the lines of decolonised ways of knowing, acting, and being.

Identifying a dilemma and proposing how it should be addressed is a way of doing philosophy of education. Identifying a dilemma is a form of thinking associated with doing philosophy. As aptly stated by Jacques Derrida (2004, p. 163), 'philosophy [of education], or rather thinking, would be this mobile non-place from which one continues or begins again . . . to ask oneself what is at stake'. And, to ask questions about a dilemma is a philosophical activity associated with thinking about a dilemma, particularly what is at stake. In this way, one appeals to a form of thinking that enables one to judge a dilemma related to its ontology, forms of knowledge, and ethical underpinnings. More specifically, philosophical thought involves a discourse of argumentation, questions, epistemology, politics, and culture that brings to light understandings of a dilemma. Considering that the dilemma under investigation is doctoral education, my interest is to find out philosophically what the thinking is behind such a form of education in Southern Africa. This form of philosophical thought is not a criticism or denouncement of a dilemma but a discourse that questions the legitimacy of a dilemma and comes up with ways to resolve the dilemma.

From my experiences promoting doctoral education over the last three decades in South Africa, I have identified at least three predicaments pertaining to doctoral education. Firstly, a predicament that relates to a lack of theoretical rigour in theses. When theses are not theoretically substantive, such texts lack understanding based on a dearth of theoretical positioning. Such theses

Preface ix

offer little in advancing theoretical ideas within particular disciplinary work. Secondly, when theses are produced to adhere to some technical requirement that work counts as a doctoral study, then such doctoral work complies procedurally with the expectations of a doctorate but, in reality, lacks deep thinking often associated with producing something innovative. Thirdly, doctoral work that does not necessarily respond to crises within society is not considered responsive to societal dystopias. It is a predicament when knowledge does not serve societal purposes and when texts are assigned to shelves without having some effect on societal change. The problem with these dilemmas in doctoral education seems to be intertwined with a notion of colonial knowledge. It is erroneously assumed that colonial knowledge is already underscored by deep theoretical thinking and, therefore, does not require further analysis. Associating colonial knowledge with finality is problematic because human thoughts cannot be considered exhaustive, as there is always more to know. However, if such knowledge is considered all-comprehensive and absolute, as may well be the case, then it is understandable that such knowledge would remain unresponsive to societal dystopias that require knowledge that is relevant and reflective.

Inasmuch as the aforementioned moral predicaments cloud the higher education system in Southern Africa, by far, the most pertinent dilemma universities face nowadays is the issue of managerialism. I have served my institution at the dean and head of department levels. I have also been exposed to a language of economic rationalism (managerialism) in which knowledge is considered a commodity and where managers insist that institutional performances should be measured against outputs produced, whether student throughput or research outputs with social impact (community engagement). Academics would hardly be considered as performing their tasks if they, for instance, do not produce publications for their institutions. In South Africa, universities are required to provide a list of all publications to the Department of Higher Education and Training (DHET), which in turn accredits such institutions with a state subsidy. In this way, the monetary survival of an institution depends on research outputs that will be accredited by the DHET for subsidy purposes. Thus, academics are under constant pressure to perform, often at the detriment of their health conditions or pedigree as scholars. For instance, one would hardly be recognised as a genuine scholar if one's outputs were at a minimal level. Annually, universities have to submit a list of publications considered as research-based work. I was quite perplexed to have heard that a book was considered more creative than research driven and hence would not be submitted for consideration for subsidy purposes. Of course, producing a text considered as creative is highly complementary. However, to claim that such a text is not research driven is to ambiguously disconnect creativity from research. If research does not reflect creativity, then such research cannot be deemed authentic. And, to discard a work on the premise that it is more creative than research orientated is to misrecognise the inextricable link between creativity and research. A closer look at the book reveals how I connected my academic travels with shifts in theoretical positioning over two decades. Considering such work as non-research and more creative is exacerbating an already contentious disconnect between creativity and research. Such managerialism is especially troubling when institutions are expected to achieve high rankings based on outputs and, if not, could face reduced funding from the state, leading to retrenchments and downsizing. Through such managerialism, Peter Scott (2015) opines that universities seem to have lost their sense of public responsibility and wider social purpose because the pressure is on them to embrace corporate values. In this regard, Richard Heller (2021) posits that unrewarding departments in universities are at risk of being sacrificed in favour of those that generate income. Even more disconcerting is when middle managers such as deans deem it necessary to consider some academic contributions as light on research as if the latter depends on the number of words used in a publication. For instance, I had an uncomfortable experience when an article to initiate was published and, subsequently, considered by our dean as not necessarily research driven. Likewise, practically in every departmental meeting at our institutions, I am confronted with the question of how many doctoral students will graduate at the end of the academic year. Fortunately, doctoral graduations have always been closely associated with my work, and throughout my professional career, I never encountered unfavourable comments about my doctoral students and their graduations. Invariably a lack of candidates for graduation would be considered as not contributing to subsidy income for the department and institution.

So what is wrong with managerialism? In the first place, academics are expected to pursue educational research on matters that interest them and the broader public. However, when institutions introduce surveillance and control measures to manage their research activities, some, if not all, of the academics' autonomy to manage their own research seems to be eroded away. The latter occurs due to an institution's drive to enhance academics' performance based on elaborate managerial structures, often at the expense of the pursuit of knowledge (McKenna, 2018). Also, managerialism institutes a workplace culture of competitiveness that often undermines colleagues' civility and collegiality (Keashly & Neuman, 2015). For instance, in the department where I work, a subtle resistance towards collegiality is often based on some academics' unwillingness to publicly share their work with colleagues based on the possibility that their ideas might be stolen and that they wish not to share their thoughts before publication. Even the thought of academics resisting public scrutiny of their work can result in such work not being given the consideration it academically deserves. The upshot is that thinking might remain parochial and truncated in and about scholarly matters.

This brings me to the question: Why are universities in (Southern) Africa under some kind of moral threat? Premised on my brief analysis of the *Doctoral Degrees National Report* (CHE, 2022), I have identified several poignant ethical concerns. Firstly, in many instances, the absence of policies and procedures relevant for doctoral studies, which include policies on recruitment, admissions, recognition of prior learning, annual progress, ethics, assessment, and doctoral work submissions. When no clear policy and procedure exist that allow students into a doctoral programme, the possibility is always there that students would gain entry into a programme for which they might not be adequately and substantively prepared. This is why some students would be registered in a doctoral programme for years without making significant progress. Often such students are the ones who are reluctant to leave the programme and, at times, blame supervisors for not attending to their concerns. Secondly, no formal agreement exists between supervisors and students at many institutions. If such agreements do not exist, a lack of accountability for both students and supervisors might be imminent. Thirdly, there seems to be no clear understanding of what students need to achieve during and after pursuing a doctorate (in reference to graduate attributes). It is a serious indictment on a doctoral programme and its coordinators when thinking about the reasons for doing such a qualification is not deemed important enough by both students and supervisors. Fourthly, tracking the progress of students is largely left unmonitored. This indicates that the work of students, if anything, is left to their own devices as if doctoral work does not require formal assessments and monitoring. Fifthly, there is a lack of adequate student (and supervisor) training in the ethics processes and research integrity required for the research project at the doctoral level. Sixthly, under-prepared students, by and large, are accepted into a doctoral programme, and seventhly, there may be an absence of formally established and well-functioning higher degree committees (or equivalent name) to oversee a doctoral programme (CHE, 2022). Of course, in some instances, such committees can also unnecessarily retard the performance of doctoral students. For instance, some students complained about the over-exuberance of such committees in providing feedback on their research proposals. On the contrary, my experience is that doctoral studies proceed more smoothly when proposals are thoroughly considered and student feedback has been substantive.

The aforementioned concerns seem to be sufficient justification to assert that university education in Africa is under some kind of moral threat, considering that the doctorate is considered an institution's 'apex qualification, and carries the expectation of international recognition' (CHE, 2022, p. 72). In the main, the concern that students do not actually understand what they ought to become during and after completion of a doctorate is what causes me to assert that university (doctoral) education in (South) Africa is under immense threat.

The question I envisage to address in this book is why (doctoral) education seems to be under threat. Usually, higher education seems to be jeopardised when particular virtues are absent or minimally practised. Virtues are those moral goods – internal goods – present in social practices that guide actions towards what can be judged as meritorious for humans (MacIntyre, 1981).

I contend that doctoral students do not consider the virtues of wonder, wandering, and whispering significant enough to pursue a doctorate. Considering that wonder involves some imaginative thought process that goes into a doctoral study that is deemed to be undervalued, then the intrinsic motivation for doing a doctorate seems to be absent. Similarly, if meandering through a formal study is not considered appropriate enough for pursuing such a qualification, then the rationale for pursuing such an inquiry is seemingly not there. And, when doctoral students do not seem to make tentative steps on their own in pursuing a doctoral qualification, the intrinsic reason for doing a doctorate is not yet present. Hence, my argument is to make a case for such virtues as enabling conditions in pursuing a doctoral university education. I have encountered many students in an education doctoral programme who failed to articulate their internal motivation for joining the programme. Many students recognised that they were in the programme for external reasons such as improving their qualifications, making themselves more eligible for promotion opportunities in the workplace, and even acquiring more respect in their communities based on their ensuing change in societal status with a doctorate. Yet many of these students were unconvincing about the internal reasons why they embarked on such a study. Consequently, I want to analyse internal goods or virtues of wonder, wander, and whisper related to pursuing higher education studies. To begin to give consideration to notions of wonder, wander, and whisper, I initiated students into doctoral studies based on their encounters with specific texts.

Which texts are enabling the pursuit of doctoral studies?

It seems odd to initiate students into the realm of doctoral studies based on prescribed texts. This is so because prescription implies that some university teachers have already decided what is good for students without the latter having some say in their education. Nevertheless, when I introduce particular texts to students, I do not intend to undermine the autonomy of students to decide for themselves. Rather, I encourage them even to scrutinise the texts I suggest they familiarise themselves with. This implies that familiarity is more prudent than prescription because if one wants to judge texts, one first needs to know something about them. In fact, a prescribed text is also an opportunity to critically engage with the work of others related to one's own intellectual pursuits. Therefore, it seems to be no harm to tell students what texts they should familiarise themselves with – that is, these texts should be subjected to critical scrutiny by readers. In preparation for doctoral studies, I have encouraged most of our students to familiarise themselves with three important texts:

Firstly, Morwenna Griffiths's (1998) compelling book, *Educational Research for Social Justice: Getting Off the Fence*, is really an invitation for prospective doctoral students, certainly in philosophy of (higher) education, to get started. Comprising three intertwined parts, the first part offers a

Preface xiii

justification for pursuing educational research in the realms of justice, fairness, and equity in (higher) education (Griffiths, 1998). What seems quite relevant is her argument that educational research 'is about taking sides and getting change in education through educational research' (Griffiths, 1998, p. 1). She premises her argument on virtues of social justice, equality, and participatory democracy in much the same way I have been advocating for many years as well. That is, when embarking on educational research at the doctoral level, students should consider their 'own personal, professional, social and political positionings' (Griffiths, 1998, p. 4). Consequently, by introducing oneself, discussing one's imaginative audience, and mentioning some relevant aspects of the historical context of the study, students endeavour 'to improve social justice through educational research, and conversely, educational research through social justice' (Griffiths, 1998, p. 5). Like Griffiths, I constantly remind my students that they are not contributing to the debate just for academic reasons but also trying to respond politically to educational practices that influence them (Griffiths, 1998). Hence, my doctoral students have been intent on educational research focusing on justice issues; educational, institutional and human agency development; and epistemology of research for social justice such as empowerment, emancipation, inclusion, and community vis-a-vis democratic citizenship education.

The second part of Griffiths's seminal work gives an account of theoretical frameworks that underscore educational research. Three actions seem to inform her advocacy for socially just educational research: openness, reflexivity, and responsibility (Griffiths, 1998). In many, if not all, of my doctoral engagements with students, I encourage them to remain open to the views of all those concerned with educational research for social justice. Openness does not mean agreeing with everything others say about social justice education but rather re-evaluating and acting upon such views' judgements (Griffiths, 1998). One should be reflexively open to others' views and to revise, where possible, such views in light of educational research for social justice. Then educational research has to be vigilant to good instead of utopian research – the latter seemingly does not exist (Griffiths, 1998). Like Griffiths, I encourage my doctoral students to become theoretically adept at working with concepts like openness, reflexivity, and responsibility as they endeavour to enlarge educational research in the field of democratic citizenship education.

The third part of Griffiths's account of educational research for social justice entails considering the 'practical consequences' of the doctoral work pursued (Griffiths, 1998, p. 127). In the main, I encourage my students to embark on critical and post-structuralist educational research in reference to the work of Iris Marion Young (1990), Jacques Rancière (1992), Seyla Benhabib (1992), Giorgio Agamben (1993), Martha Nussbaum (2001), Amy Gutmann (2003), Jacques Derrida (2004), and Jürgen Habermas (2015). What they (students) then must consider involves examining some of the educational implications of important concepts in the philosophy of (higher) education for pedagogical actions such as teaching-learning in higher education institutions. Yet central to their educational research is the notion of a reimagined idea of democratic citizenship education. In other words, students are invited to think differently about democratic citizenship education and how it relates to and potentially guides their work. The idea of rethinking democratic citizenship education is connected to a notion of decolonising higher education – that is, I encourage my students to use a contextualised notion of democratic citizenship education and examine how dominant and exclusive forms of higher education can be resisted. Thus, I encourage my students to pursue decolonised actions within their doctoral work.

Secondly, Jacques Rancière's (1992, p. 81) *On the Shores of Politics* has been significant for my understanding of doctoral supervision – one inspired by 'a community of equals'. More specifically, Rancière's (1992, p. 81) idea of a community of equals is underscored by the notion that all participants in a community have equal intelligence. In his words,

> To speak of the equality of intelligences had two basic implications: first, that every spoken or written sentence takes on meaning only if it assumes a subject whose corresponding venture permits the discernment of meaning the truth of which no pre-existing code or dictionary supplies; and second, that there are no two ways of being intelligent, that every intellectual procedure follows the same path, the part of a materiality traversed by form or meaning, and that the seat of intelligence is always the presupposed equality of a wish to say and a wish to hear.
> (Rancière, 1992, pp. 81–82)

My interest is in Rancière's (1992, p. 82) idea that every person – supervisor and student – is a speaking being and that this speaking 'would be heard'. When supervisors and students announce themselves as equals, they encourage one another to speak and be listened to. Consequently, my notion of supervision is one grounded in willing engagement. It is not enough to engage, but when supervisors and students do so willingly, there is always the possibility that what is spoken will be heard. Consequently, what students write in their texts will be read by supervisors. And equally, what supervisors comment on will be taken up by students. Such a relationship of equal reciprocity and intelligence recognises both the words of supervisors and students so that supervision becomes an exercise of a community of equals. In such a relationship, supervisors and students remain engaged where the possibility of dismissiveness and exclusion becomes impossible. The point is that, particularly in Southern Africa, where students require unbridled attention, rejection, and dismissal should not become options during supervision. It cannot be the case that a student should be left unmonitored and unattended during her doctoral journey. She should be attended to through continuous encouragement and academic opportunities to engage in seminars and writing where they practice articulation, coherent argumentation, and skilful writing. The doctorate is both a process of unconstrained meaning-making and a rigorous product of argumentation and justification in the quest to resist domination and exclusion. And one way to avoid such a situation is for students and supervisors to treat one another as intellectual equals.

Thirdly, my interest in Giorgio Agamben's (1999) *The Man Without Content* is linked to treating one's act of writing as a form of creative subjectivity. By exercising their creative subjectivity in writing, students recover their own selves, as being inside themselves to produce beautiful moments in writing – that is, becoming critically aware of words and sentences in writing that negate their arguments. Creative subjectivity becomes an act of critical reflection or judgement about one's work (Agamben, 1999). Treating one's writing as a form of creative subjectivity means that students adopt a 'poetic status' (Agamben, 1999, p. 101). This implies that they experience 'being-in-the-world' or an opening up of the world for their action and existence, thus making themselves 'capable of praxis' (Agamben, 1999, p. 101). Only when students experience poetic moments of praxis are they 'capable of willed and free activity' (Agamben, 1999, p. 101). Put differently, their writing reveals what they want to say without being hampered by the claims of others. Students are not hesitant to change their minds in writing and strive to articulate their highest expressions (Agamben, 1999). In an Agambenian way, I encourage my students to will their writing to the limit of possibility as they endeavour to bring arguments into present. They need to persist with writing, irrespective of how mediocre their arguments might appear, as long as they retain their self-critical stances. And remaining self-critical together with being in the world means that students and supervisors should remain cognisant of situations that require freedom and liberation. In Southern Africa, students and supervisors cannot remain oblivious to moments of suppression, exploitation, and domination. In my pedagogical work, I have been concerned with teaching-learning that hinders one's freedom to speak. Consequently, my supervision invariably encouraged students to critique teaching-learning that undermines freedom of articulation. Similarly, my students' theses cannot ignore social injustice and inequality issues and how the latter should be opposed. In this way, their theses became works of praxis that reflected their commitment to rectifying unjust and unequal human action.

Now that I have given some account of my students' internal reasons for pursuing doctorates, I move on to a discussion of the structural arrangement of this book.

Towards some structure

In light of the aforementioned, I have organised this book into 13 interrelated chapters with a postscript. In Chapter 1, I argue why wonder and university education ought to be inextricably intertwined. Put differently, I cannot see how wondering can be disconnected from a doctoral pursuit to analyse dilemmas. When students analyse a societal dilemma in Africa, they are encouraged to show how higher education can respond to such situations. And this implies wondering how the dilemmas could possibly be resolved. The critical stances students assume in pursuing their doctorates allow them to be open and responsive to societal predicaments. Chapter 2 offers an account of why wandering ought to be considered sacrosanct in any discourse of university education, most notably the philosophy of higher education. Wandering, as a moral virtue that enhances notions of contemplation and reflection, is considered a necessary condition in pursuing doctoral studies. The point about bringing wandering and the philosophy of higher education into play in Africa relates to how such a philosophy of higher education should wanderingly respond to predicaments on the African continent.

Chapter 3 provides a moral justification of why whispering is constitutive of any form of university education. And, when doctoral students seemingly do not whisper, they might not honour what a doctorate stands for. Again, to whisper means to initiate speech that resists undesirable situations on the African continent. Doing so whisperingly recognises the significance of speaking out unconstrainedly yet not excessively. In Chapter 4, I elucidate why university teaching-learning cannot be delinked from wondering, wandering, and whispering. Considering that doctoral education represents plausible teaching-learning in African higher education, any detachment from imaginative pursuits would be detrimental to a doctorate in any case. Chapter 5 offers a moral account of why the virtues of wondering, wandering, and whispering are so important for advancing ethical human encounters among students and supervisors. The argument is that human encounters ought to be constituted by ethical demands if such encounters were to manifest as morally plausible in cultivating doctoral pursuits.

Chapter 6 provides some justification for why student supervision ought to be considered a moral exercise of democratic citizenship. To associate doctoral supervision with democratic citizenship education in the first place is to announce such a form of education's political and moral intent. It also speaks to an agenda of decolonising higher education in Africa, based on the view that cultivating an emancipatory form of democratic citizenship education invariably accentuates the need to decolonise higher education. Chapter 7 shows why doctoral education ought to be linked to the cultivation of cosmopolitan justice. If doctoral education cannot be about connecting with others in their otherness, there would be no moral point in such a qualification. In Chapter 8, I examine doctoral supervision in relation to a notion of critique. It is through critique that supervisors and students engage rigorously in the pursuit of doctoral completion. Here, completion does not imply finality but rather a moment in temporal time when the qualification has been examined and considered credible enough for publication.

In Chapter 9, I argue why doctoral education should become a pedagogical space for profanation and play. Through profanation and play, more pedagogical, ethical, and epistemological opportunities are carved out for doctorates to be really meaningful to the public moral good. Chapter 10 provides some narrative of my own doctoral experiences and why wondering, wandering, and whispering manifested in such experiences. I frame my personal doctoral actions along the lines of wondering-wandering-whispering to lay claim that embarking on such a qualification is a genuinely epistemological and moral-political action. Put differently, my doctoral journey represents a pathway to authentically decolonise higher education in Southern Africa. It is a pedagogical form of resistance intertwined with moments of contestation and conflict to ensure that autonomy and freedom are retained and advanced in the interest of cultivating decolonised practices within African higher education. In Chapter 11, I provide an account of a university, specifically invoking three types of universities that informed my thinking: a reasoned university, a democratic university, and an ubuntu university. In Chapter 12, I offer some conceptual-pragmatic framework of how doctoral supervision can be actualised in its potentiality. I am attracted to the notion of an ubuntu university that also provides three analysis points for which doctoral supervision should unfold: autonomous, iterative, and restorative action. In Chapter 13, I argue that doctoral education in South Africa seems to be remiss of wonder, wander, and whisper. Hence, I posit that doctoral programmes in the country need to be reconceptualised. If any doctoral pursuit does not consider wonder, wander, and whisper as legitimate reasons for wanting to embark on a doctoral study, then such qualifications remain in peril.

Summary

This book does not claim to provide a utopian perspective of how doctoral education and its supervision should occur. On the contrary, it represents a reflective moment in my thinking on why and how doctoral inquiries could become more tenable from an epistemological, moral, and political perspective, while being more responsive to the times of the day, especially in Africa, where decolonisation and decoloniality should remain emancipatory acts of moral, political, and epistemological pursuits. I merely share some of my experiences in doctoral supervision, articulated in theoretically and pragmatically acceptable ways, with ramifications for its possible practical and moral implementation. It might be that some of my readers will learn from my experiences or, conversely, subvert some of the claims I proffer throughout the book. I have no intention to claim that there is some utopian practice on doctoral education that I have emulated. Rather, my analyses represent reflections and (de)constructions of understandings in and about doctoral education and supervision perhaps not considered previously. I could have commenced with my narrative on my personal doctoral experiences as an introductory chapter. However, I decided to conclude with my story in an attempt to corroborate some of the theoretical-cum-practical positions I have argued for in this book. In no small way does my narrative provide some moral justification for my choice of ideas and concepts used throughout the book. So let me begin.

References

Agamben, G. (1993). *The coming community*. University of Minnesota Press.
Agamben, G. (1999). *The man without content* (G. Albert, Trans.). Stanford University Press.
Benhabib, S. (1992). *Situating the self: Gender, community, and postmodernism in contemporary politics*. Routledge.
CHE. (2022). *National review of South African doctoral qualifications 2020–2021: Doctoral degrees national report*. Author.
Derrida, J. (2004). *Eyes of the university: Right to philosophy 2*. Stanford University Press.
Griffiths, M. (1998). *Educational research for social justice: Getting off the fence*. Open University Press.
Gutmann, A. (2003). *Identity in democracy*. Princeton University Press.
Habermas, J. (2015). *The structural transformation of the public sphere*. Polity Press.
Harris, C. (2004). How did colonialism dispossess? Comments from an edge of empire. *Annals of the Association of American Geographers, 94*(1), 165–182.
Heller, R. F. (2021). *The problem with universities today*. Springer.
Keashly, L., & Neuman, J. H. (2015). Faculty experiences with bullying in higher education. *Adm Theor Praxis, 32*(1), 48–70. https://doi.org/10.2753/ATP1084-1806320103.
MacIntyre, A. (1981). *After virtue*. Duckworth.
McClintock, A. (1994). The angel of progress: Pitfalls of the term postmodernism. In F. Barker, P. Hulme, & M. Iversen (Eds.), *Colonial discourse/postcolonial theory*. Manchester University Press.
McKenna, S. (2018, March). Here are five signs that universities are turning into corporations. *The Conversation*. https://theconversation.com/here-are-five-signs-that-universities-are-turning-into-corporations-93100
Nussbaum, M. C. (2001). *Upheavals of thought: The intelligence of emotions*. Cambridge University Press.
Rancière, J. (1992). *On the shore of politics*. Verso.
Scott, P. (2015). Universities are losing are losing their sense of public responsibility and social purpose. *The Guardian*. www.theguardian.com/education/2015/jan/06/public-universities-becoming-corporate-losing-social-purpose
Waghid, Y., Terblanche, J., Shawa, L., Hungwe, J., Waghid, F., & Waghid, Z. (Eds.). (2023). *Towards and ubuntu university: African higher education re-imagined*. Palgrave-Macmillan.
Young, I. M. (1990). *Justice and the politics of difference*. Princeton University Press.
Young, I. M. (2005). De-centering the project of global democracy. In D. Levy, M. Pensky, & J. Torbey (Eds.), *In old Europe, new Europe, core Europe* (pp. 153–159). Verso.

1 University education and the quest to wonder

Introduction

University education is as much a practice constituted by epistemological, social, and political virtues as a moral action. Talking about university education as a virtue in the first place implies that such a form of education is important in exercising humans' moral capacities – that is, virtue is intertwined with an act of morality (Krisjánsson, 2013). Simply put, a university education is also a moral action. In practising university education, students and teachers exercise virtues such as discipline, selflessness, determination, dependability, reliability, trustworthiness, loyalty, and reasonableness (Krisjánsson, 2013). Thus, exercising virtues is tantamount to embarking on some kind of moral action because people are concerned with exercising good aspects of life (Waghid, 2014). Much of my work in university education centres around the virtue of reasonableness. To be reasonable implies that we are prepared to offer some justification for why we think something is possible and why it might not be prudent to undermine it. Reasonableness is connected to providing some moral justification for why something can be considered authentic. For instance, it would be reasonable to claim that most, if not all, doctoral students consider thinking as necessary for the arguments justified in texts. Thinking unfolds in many forms, of which wonder(ing) represents a specific form of thinking in the same way reflection coheres with thinking. To associate wondering with thinking is a recognition that when one wonders about something, the possibility is always there that one gives thought to that something. In other words, wondering is thoughtful action, that is, what has been given thought to happen because of one's wondering. For instance, to wonder about the state of higher education in Southern African universities is to consider such education. The very act of wondering is a commitment to thinking that involves reflection, understanding, and criticism. So let us analyse wonder as a form of thinking that we presume ought to be part of doctoral work.

What does it mean to wonder? I am attracted to Giorgio Agamben's (1999) depiction of wonder, which he elucidates in the context of art. For him, any work of art requires acts of wonder associated with ingeniousness, rarity, subtlety, curiosity, and discernment – that is, moral virtues of thinking (Agamben, 1999). The act of wonder would hardly be present if artworks are not done by being imaginative, unexpected (eccentric), and insightful or perceptive – referred to by Agamben as doing art for its own sake. I examine such a notion of wonder in relation to university doctoral education. My reason for pursuing such an investigation is to ascertain why wonder ought to be linked morally to doctoral inquiry and if there is something in and about wonder that justifies it being a concept without which a doctorate cannot be pursued. Put differently, I shall endeavour to analyse whether wonder is both a necessary and enabling condition of doctoral education and supervision. My own philosophical work has always been prefaced by the question: I wonder why this concept is important and how it fits in our theses. It is questions like these that make me wonder about the moral significance of wonder itself.

That wonder has moral importance and is attested to by an inquiry into whether the African philosophy of higher education, for instance, needs decolonisation. Students and I, engaged in the African philosophy of higher education, wonder whether such a philosophy is reflective enough to bring about decolonised thinking. To think in a decolonised way means that one opposes the racist colonised undertones that seem to embody a philosophy of higher education. Decolonised thinking wants to oppose the prejudices and misconceptions that seem to underscore a philosophy of higher education in Southern Africa.

Wonder and university education

It would be quite audacious to articulate a university's function as not serving the interests of knowledge, considering that the literature is replete with claims about the public reasonableness of the modern university concerning the cultivation of knowledge. For several eminent theorists, a university is 'a forum of debate about culture, politics, and intellectual life' (Altbach, 2007, p. xx) – a space to develop 'more just, democratic, cosmopolitan futures' (Rizvi, 2007, p. x) and a place of 'reason, judgement, integrity, impartiality, truth, knowledge, disinterestedness, critical dialogue, careful inquiry and cognitive authority' (Barnett, 2016, p. 5). Although the aforementioned views of a university resonate with the advancement of knowledge vis-à-vis the quest for public reasonableness, it does not specifically accentuate the need for wonder in and through university education, more specifically doctoral studies. To think of a university as an intellectual space for democratic politics, critical engagement, and cosmopolitanism, such noble aims or moral actions do not necessarily make us think of a university as a place where wonder ought to be enacted. Why is wonder so important in depicting what a university ought to do? If one looks at wonder as a human capacity to be imaginative, eccentric, and perceptive, then such cognitive capabilities would be apposite to (re) consider university education along the lines of democratic politics, cultural innovations, and cosmopolitan futures. Put differently, through wonder, such purposes of a university would have been much better thought through.

Agamben (1999, p. 34) specifically contrives wonder as that human capability that puts human thought gracefully and indistinctly in tune with a divine presence. Grace seems to be associated with agile thinking, whereby ideas flow with a sense of fluency, whereas indistinctiveness appears to be linked to indeterminate thought that intimates thinking can yet become clear. Thus, when thinking is graceful and indistinct, it raises the possibility that ideas can emerge without being suppressed indefinitely. When human thought encounters a divine presence, it creates the potential for such thinking to be morally beautiful and engaging. Consequently, the act of wondering in graceful and indeterminate ways opens up the possibility for human speech to become riveting and passionate to the extent that a person can become creatively and morally thoughtful. When university teachers and students become creative, their thoughts would propel them into becoming graceful and passionate thinkers concerned with morally engaging one another in idiosyncratic ways. Such is the art of wonder so that university education does not merely remain conventional and familiar but that educational experiences become unfamiliar, suspicious, or sceptical.

Why is scepticism so necessary in university education, more specifically doctoral studies? Education is an encounter that exists among humans. Human encounters – people engaging with one another – are often lived out in the face of doubt. This implies that human encounters (actions) in the face of doubt are often inconclusive (Cavell, 1979). So a university education cannot be considered conclusive or without doubt, as that would be the end of such education. That is, there would be no point in engaging one another in encounters. For this reason, Stanley Cavell (1979, p. 440) is right when he avers that humans live their scepticism when they do not completely know one another or conceive the other from the other's point of view. By implication, if human encounters remain inconclusive and endless, as Cavell puts it, their education would be underscored by suspicion – that is, strangeness, uncertainty, and doubt. In this way, human encounters remain sceptical because they (humans) would be imperfectly known to one another (Cavell, 1979). As aptly stated by Cavell (1979, p. 447), living one's scepticism concerning others is a matter of encountering the other with 'radical doubt'. In reference to university education, scepticism becomes an experience of the other with doubt and uncertainty that there is still much to know or not to know from human encounters with one another. Here, we are thinking of doctoral encounters in which supervisors and students sceptically look at one another's claims about humanity and social life, about accepting and denying one another's points of view on such matters. In a way, scepticism seems to enhance humans' sense of wonder because they do not exactly know one another's claims on matters that either illuminate or deny their speculative thoughts on human possibilities. In a nutshell, scepticism is an instance of wonder because nothing about human relations can ever be completely known. According to Cavell (1979, p. 443), 'all anyone knows or could know is what I am able to show them of myself'. In this way, one is invariably known imperfectly to others about which others and oneself continue or not to wonder. Similarly, supervisors and doctoral students would get to know one another based on how they present themselves in educational encounters.

What follows from the analysis mentioned earlier of wonder is that the insertion of radical doubt into understandings of human encounters portrays such encounters as ambivalent, inconclusive, and uncertain. Considering that humans (supervisors and students) are at the centre of doctoral education, their encounters cannot be about attaining certainty and completeness, for pursuing these alone would render education conclusive, which it is not. There is always more to know and encounter, and for university education to reach closeness and certainty would be catastrophic for any ensuing forms of intellectual inquiry. There cannot be an end to knowledge and human encounters, for that would be the end of human life on earth, specifically their educational encounters. For university education to remain a genuine form of education, it is to remain wondrously educated in the face of doubt, as Cavell would put it.

To continue on this path of pursuing a university education in the face of wonder, I next examine the perspective of aesthetic judgement and its implications for university education.

Aesthetic judgement and university education

In contrast to Kant's depiction of critical judgement, which relies on a solid rational foundation, aesthetic judgement seems to rely more on a mystical intuition inherent in the judgement of artistic beauty (Agamben, 1999). Aesthetic judgement seems to be underscored by four characteristics of beauty, namely disinterested satisfaction, universality apart from concepts, purposiveness without purpose, and normality without norm (Agamben, 1999, p. 42). This makes aesthetic judgement a self-critical stance towards something which gives rise to its negation (Agamben, 1999). Thus, judging art aesthetically means assuming a critical stance towards its negation – that is, non-art. Consequently, Agamben (1999, p. 49) posits that aesthetic judgement distinguishes art 'from its shadow and authenticity from inauthenticity'. That is, to judge a work (of art) means to measure it against its negation or otherness – a matter of reversing or searching for an impossible meaning (Agamben, 1999, p. 51). So aesthetically judging university education means to measure it against what is not university education – a matter of bringing university education back to its opposite, dissolving it into non-university education. Aesthetically judging university education, then, means juxtaposing it against what does not count as university education, thus 'becoming aware of its shadow' (Agamben, 1999, p. 50). In this way, a critical reflection on university education passes through an aesthetic judgement of what does not count as university education, which requires some semblance of wonder in its pursuit. When one wonders about university education, aesthetic judgement enables one to come up with thoughts on what does not constitute university education – its opposite – which invariably enlarges one's understanding of such a form of education.

Whereas critical judgement represents a justification based on why university education is what it is, aesthetic judgement negates non-university education, thus rendering a more intuitive notion of what university education involves. The idea of searching for so-called best practices of university education does not necessarily mean that such a form of education is authentic. Rather, identifying and wondering about forms of non-university education could illuminate an understanding of the practice. Agamben (1999) opines that in searching for good artwork, one needs to consider mediocre and bad works of art. This means that any aesthetic judgement on what makes for good university education implies measuring it against its negation. For instance, if one wonders about the good university (philosophy of) higher education, one can judge such a form of education against the non-philosophy of higher education – a matter of wondering whether it is aesthetically beautiful or alien. Here, I think of several non-philosophy of higher education courses offered at universities in South Africa to consider more authentic versions of the discipline. Similarly, good doctoral education should be compared with its negation, which does not constitute good doctoral studies. The notion of decolonisation and its negated form of colonised knowledge are also of particular interest. If one wants to ascertain why decolonised knowledge should be considered necessary in cultivating doctoral education, it seems feasible to analyse why exclusionary and hegemonic colonised knowledge subverts doctoral inquiry. If colonisation is meant to deny humans' humanity, then decolonisation aims to free humans from such oppressive acts.

Next, I show how wondering was realised related to some students' doctoral work. Considering that students' theses, except one that had been converted into book form, have not been publicised, I have decided to provide pseudonyms for the authors of these theses under discussion although these theses do appear on an institutional repository. I do not embark on critical appraisals but rather point out how particular action concepts like wonder, wander, whisper, ethical encounters, democratic citizenship, cosmopolitan justice, profanation, and play were actualised in their potentialities.

Provoking students to wonder: the examples of Frank, Neville, Bart, and Harold

Frank, Neville, Bart, and Harold were all registered for a doctorate during the same years. All of their theses involved philosophical analyses of concepts pertaining to school governance, teacher education, university transformation, and knowledge actions, respectively. They were not provided with ready-made themes or topics but were summoned to wonder about specific topics. If students are expected to wonder, it does not make sense to always tell them what they need to do. In quite autonomous ways, they were attracted to ideas and concepts they had been involved with at the time. Frank chose to write about school governance because he was a governor at a local school and thought that something had to be done to improve governance at the school. For him, the lack of plausible governance at former marginalised schools under investigation posed a moral dilemma to those involved in schooling. Consequently, he was attracted to critical educational theory and its links to empowerment and liberation and used it throughout his thesis as a framework of analysis. He was always intent on thinking again and again – a matter of wondering – about school governance improvement and consequently made an argument for the use of democratic citizenship education as a way to enhance thinking about school governance in reference to Jürgen Habermas's (2003) analysis of the concept.

It would be unwise to assert that Frank did not wonder about his doctoral work. Instead, his sense of wonder came through, especially when he relooked at the idea of school governance in line with democratic citizenship education to give his thesis an epistemological, moral, and political bias. Throughout his doctoral work, Frank was adamant that a reconceptualised notion of school governance attuned to a liberal notion of democratic citizenship education could help school governors and educators to think differently about governance that invariably influences school management. Although Frank adapted a Habermasian notion of democratic citizenship education related to his understanding of school governance, he did not always convince how the notion guided a renewed understanding of school management. Nevertheless, he was provoked to wonder about such a notion which he seemed to have responded to adequately during his viva voce. Wondering was close to Frank's thinking, which juxtaposed his understanding of school governance against the cultivation of democratic citizenship education in previously marginalised schools where gang violence and intimidation held sway. He wondrously disrupted skewed understandings of school governance using critical educational theory.

Neville was persuaded by the idea that teacher education in South African schools ought to be reconsidered in light of the normative virtues of teacher education – professionalism, integrity, and ethical action. In quite a wonderous way, he scrutinised teacher professionalism, integrity, and ethical action based on a neo-Aristotelian notion of virtue in reference to the seminal work of Alasdair MacIntyre (1981). What makes his work intellectual and vigorous is his reconsideration of moral virtue and how teacher education should be relooked at in a non-dichotomous way vis-à-vis theory and practice. He was not prepared to only use MacIntyre's work uncritically but actually adapted the latter's interpretation of virtue to come up with his own notion of the concept. His main claim relates to considering teacher education as a moral virtue that can engender ethical action within the teaching profession. Yet Neville did not convince regarding his explication of teacher norms and values as he seemed to have intimated that such norms and values of teacher education should be exercised universally – an idea that happens to be incongruent with a notion of indigeneity – that is, thinking of values of teacher education as relevant to the context in which teachers work. However, his argument for ethical teacher autonomy as a response to a normativised notion of teacher education seems novel in the sense that it relates to a decolonial enactment of autonomy whereby teachers assert their ethical commitment towards change in South African teacher education. His work enhanced a decolonised notion of teacher education that opposes irrational and finalised ideas of the practice.

Unlike Frank and Neville, Bart was mainly concerned with analysing institutional transformation related to a renewed interpretation of government legislation in South Africa. For him, transformation was a sui generis term that can only be reduced to permanent change towards socially just and moral action. What is quite wonderous about the use of this concept is that it involves ethical action that subverts notions of inequality, unfreedom, inaccess, and exclusion. He drew on Habermas's notion of the public sphere to argue why institutional transformation ought to be reconsidered according to tenets of democratic action and citizenship responsibilities. What is quite interesting about Bart's thesis is that he seems to make a moral justification for philosophical analyses of university transformation based on empirical inquiries at three institutions in the surrounding areas of Cape Town. Although Bart's doctoral work did not explicitly mention the decolonisation of higher education, his work invariably related to decolonised actions pertaining to unfreedom, inaccess, and injustice within higher education. In a way, his emphasis on the democratisation of higher education in Southern Africa is, in fact, an appeal to decolonised action within higher education.

In contrast to Bart, Harold was concerned with knowledge (re)organisation, which he proffers is only possible through democratic action. He averred that if universities were to become more credible knowledge producers, they ought to be linked to the cultivation of autonomous and collaborative persons interested in advancing learning. Hence, for him, learning was an act of knowledge creation – a clear reference to wondering about claims of knowledge. Also, he was equally interested in the notion of co-learning, which seems to connect conceptually with an idea of citizenship education as a co-responsible practice to be enacted by autonomous persons. His work seemed to be silent on the decolonisation of higher education, although knowledge (re)creation could be conceived as an act of decoloniality.

In all instances earlier, students were provoked to think for themselves and to wonder about the arguments they proffered. Any form of thesis writing devoid of wondering and credible argumentation would do little to advance viable doctoral work. Equally, the aforementioned doctoral theses were also about cultivating defensible moral actions among teachers and students.

8 *University education and the quest to wonder*

And, for them to engage in deliberative encounters they ought to have internalised virtues of co-existence, co-responsibility, and co-learning.

Summary

University education cannot be practised without wonder as the latter situates its grace and distinctness morally. Likewise, university education should not be exercised without scepticism as that enhances its (un)clarity. Yet sceptical doubt lends itself to a form of negation – a matter of searching for the opposites of things that could render university education aesthetically defensible. Without exercising aesthetic judgement, university teachers and students would find it difficult to pursue a sense of wonder and scepticism so necessary to ensure the inconclusiveness and ambivalence that ought to be associated with university education. Wondering students engage gracefully, distinctly, and aesthetically with doctoral work that lays a pedagogical platform to decolonise university (doctoral) education.

References

Agamben, G. (1999). *The man without content* (G. Albert, Trans.). Stanford University Press.
Altbach, P. G. (2007). The underlying realities of higher education in the 21st century. In P. G. Altbach & P. McGill (Eds.), *Higher education in the new century: Global challenges and innovative ideas* (pp. xiv–xxii). Sense Publishers.
Barnett, R. (2016). *Understanding the university: Institution, idea, possibilities*. Routledge.
Cavell, S. (1979). *The claim of reason: Wittgenstein, skepticism, morality, and tragedy*. Oxford University Press.
Habermas, J. (2003). *The future of human nature* (W. Rehg, M. Pensky, & H. Beister, Trans.). Polity Press.
Krisjánsson, K. (2013, March 22–24). Ten myths about character, virtue and virtue education – plus three well-founded misgivings. Proceedings of Annual Conference of Philosophy of Education Society of Great Britain, New College, pp. 22–38.
MacIntyre, A. (1981). *After virtue: A study in moral theory*. Duckworth.
Rizvi, F. (2007). Foreword. In M. A. Peters (Ed.), *Knowledge economy, development and the future of higher education* (pp. vii–x). Sense Publishers.
Waghid, Y. (2014). Curriculum and moral debates: On virtue education and multicultural integration. In P. du Preez & C. Reddy (Eds.), *Curriculum studies: Visions and imaginings* (pp. 76–90). Pearson.

2 Wandering and university education

In pursuit of poiesis, praxis, and rhythm

Introduction

If university education cannot do without wonder, scepticism, and aestheticism, then equally, it cannot be remiss of wandering (roaming). To wonder is to think and rethink educational matters. However, when one (re)thinks, one often travels on a cognitive pathway of discovering and justifying why things are what they are and ought to be. It is when one moves from place to place, one embarks on wandering. Throughout my academic career, I have wandered from city to city, presenting papers as far as Kyoto, Seoul, Melbourne, Waikato, and Kuala Lumpur on one side of the globe, to Oslo, Hamburg, Konya, Granada, London, New York, San Diego, and New Orleans on the other side of the globe. Visits to these cities and many others have often been inspired by my wandering thoughts in and about the philosophy of higher education related to cultivating a communitarian understanding of democratic citizenship education (Waghid, 2021). During academic visits to many cities in the world, my wandering often lured me into new thoughts about a philosophy of higher education. Consequently, it is not surprising that my wandering prompted me to (re)construct an African philosophy of higher education based on three considerations: firstly, a notion of cosmopolitan *ubuntu* that accentuates humans' capacities to recognise one another in their commonalities and differences and their co-living; secondly, an understanding that humans should be bound together by cosmopolitan caring; and thirdly, that humans should engage in iterations that can engender agreement and dissent that would encourage them to become intellectual activists (Waghid, 2021). Such a philosophy of higher education only became possible due to my meandering thoughts.

In the previous chapter, the argument was made for an uncertain and inconclusive university education (doctoral studies). Yet such a form of university education cannot be possible only through the cognitive act of wonder. To only wonder about university education would not get us very far but, instead, limit our thinking in and about university education to acts of surprise and amazement. Rather, as will be argued in this chapter, wandering, as the

DOI: 10.4324/9781032715872-2

10 *Wandering and university education*

meandering pursuit of knowledge, should also become endemic to any form of university education. My reason for linking wandering to education is that the notion not only is inextricably related to moral action (Szpunar et al., 2013) but extends into doing something morally worthwhile about what we wonder about. Wandering is considered a moral action according to which university education can most appropriately be enacted as an extension of wondering (Szpunar et al., 2013). It is to such a discussion that we now turn to.

Wandering and education: reconsidering poiesis, praxis, and rhythm

For Giorgio Agamben (1999), poiesis (producing) means to bring something into presence creatively and artistically that was not in existence before. A person of poiesis knows that she caused something to appear without that something having existed previously. In this way, her wandering was not some aimless exercise but rather a creative exercise of having brought something that did not exist into her presence. Poiesis implies that the study of the philosophy of higher education cannot be some meaningless and purposeless exercise but rather an act of wandering that remains radically open to new ways of thinking, writing, and speaking of education. In this regard, Igor Jasinski (2018, p. 96) is correct when he posits that philosophy of (higher) education (as wandering) involves 'coming up with ever new constellations of thinking about education in the process' – a matter of producing insights not considered previously. For instance, the literature is replete with exhortations about democratic citizenship education, as noted by Wiel Veugelers (2019). For him, democratic citizenship education involves adapting, developing an individual's independence and critical thought, and learning to live together in deliberation and diversity towards activism. Yet, in further analysing the concept, it was found that democratic citizenship education theory is also underscored by an act of decoloniality. Such a view of democratic citizenship education would invariably enhance a theory of higher education. Considering decoloniality as an instance of democratic citizenship education theory would be tantamount to producing a new insight into the fray. The point is that framing democratic citizenship education along the lines of iterations, recognition of the other, and cultivation of human freedom is to announce a particular form of education. However, when such an understanding of education is extended into the realm of decoloniality, it immediately invokes a notion of resistance and inclusion.

Likewise, higher education as wandering involves praxis enunciated as 'productive doing' whereby humans will their actions to their limit (Agamben, 1999, p. 74). When humans will their actions, the possibility is always there that such actions would have some practical implications for activities pursued. The emphasis here is on wilful productive action, such as developing an educational curriculum for a university programme. Now this education curriculum in itself cannot be considered actualised, for that would imply that the curriculum is complete and cannot be amended. However, if an education curriculum were to be regarded as potentialised, then the possibility is that such a curriculum can be amended and improved. In this way, productive doing (praxis) remains an enactment of will not towards some final or predetermined goal but a process that remains open to possible outcomes – described by Agamben as a curriculum in suspension or wandering (Agamben, 1999). Here, I am specifically thinking of producing a doctorate. As students continue writing on their topics, they do not consider the outcomes of their writing as finalised pieces of work. Rather, these pieces of writing are considered passages that could be tampered with so that more insightful meanings could be procured. This does not mean supervisors merely comment cryptically on students' work without justifying their concerns. Instead, comments should be about opening up more opportunities for writing to become more feasible. In this way, praxis as an act of wandering offers more opportunities to improve pieces of writing.

Agamben (1999, p. 100) describes rhythm both 'to hold back, to suspend, and to hand over, to present, to offer'. In this way, to wander means to introduce into one's path 'an interruption in the incessant flow of instants' (Agamben, 1999, p. 99). It is this stop or holding back together with giving or advancing ahead that gives wandering human action its ecstatic hurling out into rhythm. Educationally speaking, studying rhythmically consists 'in an oscillation, a back and forth between a state of bewilderment and lucidity, between some kind of directionality and a complete lack thereof' (Jasinski, 2018, p. 36). When doctoral writing subscribes to rhythmic action, ideas would be continuously reconsidered based on interruptions in the fluency of writing that allows one to hold back, reconsider, and then advance again. Doctoral thesis writing subjected to rhythmic action would involve a free flow of ideas and sentences that would be interrupted only for supervisors and students to reflect on the writing before students would again hurl forth with their writing.

On Masasa, Nellie, Gail, Igor, and Celia's rhythmic educational moments

I now show how poiesis, praxis, and rhythm as instances of wandering appeared to have manifested in relation to the doctoral work of some students. In his effort to articulate a defence of a liberal notion of higher education commensurate with autonomy in Africa, Masasa was concerned with bringing something into presence – that is, an understanding that liberality can co-exist with autonomous higher education. Equally, he was insistent that such a relation could be enacted to its limit so that what is presented is no longer what was conceived previously – that is, new insights would have emerged about African higher education. He rhythmically pursued his writing by using interruption to rethink possibilities in and about the commensurability between liberality and autonomy. At first, Masasa pursued his writing and interrupted himself on advice from his supervisor to rethink some of his thoughts, only to continue later again once he made sense of what was being said. Like Masasa, Nellie's concern was to show that democratic education and school governance ought to be looked at according to poiesis, praxis, and rhythm. Through disrupted forms of poiesis and praxis, she showed how defensible forms of school governance are grounded in democratic educational theory and how they can enhance teaching-learning in public schools. In turn, Gail was adamant that educational leadership should be constituted by a paradigm of democratic citizenship education. Using disrupted forms of poiesis and praxis, she rhythmically showed how multiple forms of educational leadership manifest in schools and, conversely, how schooling in post-apartheid South Africa reinforces more tenable forms of educational leadership often couched in the form of transformational leadership.

Igor's thesis took issue with a notion of outcomes-based education, which he argued is not transformative enough to enact change in the South African schooling system. In quite a rhythmic fashion, Igor showed how education as outcomes undermines any attempt to produce authentic schooling, and through a process of suspension and advancement, he offered possibilities that seem to go against any form of defensible education, which led him to proffer that outcomes-based education is untransformative. In contrast to Igor, Celia's thesis showed that democratic education in Namibian schools ought to be deepened if any form of legitimate transformation were to manifest. She showed how the virtues of deep democracy can impact in reference to the work of Iris Marion Young (2002), authentic schooling specifically related to cultivating an expansive form of engagement among teachers and learners. What seemed to come through in Masasa, Nellie, Gail, Igor, and Celia's doctoral work is that writing should be rhythmic. If students do not suspend their writing willingly and conscientiously, they will be unable to see certain things about their theses. When they again resume writing after some interruption, they could more cogently articulate claims as they would have been incapable of doing had they not temporarily interrupted their doctoral writing.

A reflective moment on my own rhythmic experiences

On attending the 2006 International Network of Philosophers of Education Conference in Malta, I happened to present my paper on 'Education as friendship'. After my presentation, Gert Biesta and Barbara Thayer-Bacon advised me to rethink my understanding of friendship in education based on the notion of risk-taking. Previously, I was persuaded that friendship in education is constituted by deliberative encounters whereby people articulate themselves, listen to what others have to say, and talk back to others in (dis)agreement. They reminded me that following a Derridian notion of friendship, I can also expand such a notion of friendship to one of taking risks – that is, only if people are encouraged to take risks in the presence of one another, the possibility for genuine friendship might ensue. It was then that my thinking on friendship fluctuated rhythmically between friendship as a form of iteration and one of riskful action.

Since visiting Malta, I have become more adept at looking beyond notions I wonder about. Engaging in rhythmic action eventually inspired me to reconsider my understanding of democratic citizenship education and the philosophy of higher education today. Upon wandering, the possibility is always there that one would rethink and reconsider concepts differently and even in an expanded form. Until recently, I have analysed and elucidated a notion of *ubuntu*. I have stepped back from my previous understanding of *ubuntu* to one that embraces a notion of cosmopolitan justice in much the same way I have rethought (rhythmically) a Derridian understanding of friendship in education.

Summary

Wandering can be enacted in the context of university doctoral education whereby participants (teachers or supervisors and students) pursue practices such as poiesis, praxis, and rhythm. Whereas poiesis requires university teachers (supervisors) and students to produce knowledge in creative ways, praxis considers them as actionable beings whereby they endeavour to embrace a university curriculum in productive ways – that is, acting towards potential outcomes rather than ready-made ones. Finally, wandering rhythmically causes teachers and students to interrupt their knowledge pursuits as they work towards bewilderment and directionality.

References

Agamben, G. (1999). *The man without content* (G. Albert, Trans.). Stanford University Press.
Jasinski, I. (2018). *Giorgio Agamben: Education without ends*. Springer.
Szpunar, K., Moulton, S., & Schacter, D. (2013). Mind wandering and education: From the classroom to online learning. *Frontiers in Psychology, 4*(1), 1–7. https://doi.org/10.3389/fpsyg.2013.00495.
Veugelers, W. (Ed.). (2019). *Education for democratic intercultural citizenship*. Brill.
Waghid, Y. (2021). *Mildly twists and turns: A philosopher's memoir*. SUN Press.
Young, I. M. (2002). *Inclusion and democracy*. Oxford University Press.

3 Whispering as studious and playful university education

Introduction

One of the stark criticisms of doctoral education in (Southern) Africa relates to the under-preparedness of students for such studies and the lack of financial and supervisory support for such students (CHE, 2022). As outrageous as such criticisms might appear, one would not expect a doctoral candidate to be under-prepared for such studies after so many opportunities to have acquired capacities and skills to pursue such a formal qualification, at least having been exposed to research at a master's level, the issue is real. For me, doctoral students seemed to not have gained sufficient insight into the infancy of a research language that holds them back from pursuing a doctorate. Often doctoral proposals are inadequate and invariably require major revisions regarding vague research questions and methodological inconsistencies. Inadequate doctoral proposals do not augur well for the actual doctorate itself. At this level, incoherence and a lack of argumentation are serious concerns tied to often unclear articulations and pedantic expressions. Consequently, in this chapter, we argue that doctoral participants need to embark on the act of whispering. To whisper means to speak softer because it is expected that doctoral students still have much to learn as they embark on their research journeys. When doctoral students offer subdued understandings of their work, there seems to be no harm in doing so. After all, doctoral students are in their infancy regarding educational research.

On infancy, potentiality, and the doctorate – a matter of whispering

My argument in defence of infancy is linked to the idea that initial doctoral education should not be linked to producing flawless texts. Doctoral writing, in particular, is a matter of taking small steps to pursue something defensible and not error-free. Students grow into a doctorate and cannot always get it right instantly. That is, they are initiated into a doctorate. Agamben (2007) considers infancy as a state of being unable to speak – a matter of not being fully human as yet. When humans cannot speak, the possibility invariably exists that they can speak in the future or not speak. As Jasinski (2018, p. 26) so aptly reminds us: '[T]he experience of infancy allows us to stay open to (the possibility for) new and different ways of speaking (and, thus, thinking and doing)'. As embodied beings, humans either can speak or must still develop a language to speak. If so, they are in a state of infancy, that is, experiencing 'the potentiality of language' (Jasinski, 2018, p. 29). The significance of Agamben's (2007) notion of infancy is that humans during infancy develop the potential to speak through articulation and communication. However, because of being in a state of infancy, their language is suspended, thus making them unable to speak.

Showing a potential to speak implies that they can speak but not competently yet and hence remain in a state of infancy. Concerning doctoral education, students are said to be in a state of infancy when they are not yet equipped with a language to articulate themselves – having a doctoral voice perhaps – and to communicate their arguments, at least through writing. Thus, when students are said to be underprepared to write their theses, they do not yet possess the language of thesis writing that they require to expedite their task. Their infancy in doctoral studies corroborates why they do not yet have a voice to articulate their arguments or claims about this or that. In this way, students experience infancy or what Agamben (2007, p. 54) refers to as a 'silence of the [doctoral] subject'. It is a 'wordless experience' that prevents the infant doctoral student from possessing a language of research. And, when doctoral students are not yet speaking, they do not have a language to articulate their thoughts and speech. Doctoral students unequipped with a language do not have speech, as Agamben (2007) posits.

Without transcending infancy, doctoral students would not be in a position to study. In other words, without learning to speak, students would be unable to communicate with others, articulate themselves, and write their theses – a matter of pursuing their studies. As Jasinski (2018) avers, students would not be radically open to content and directionality because they have not transcended their infancy which involves, as Agamben (1995, p. 64) so aptly reminds us, 'long hours spent roaming among books'. For Agamben (1995), immersing oneself interminably (sustainedly) in study opens up infinite possibilities. As he puts it,

> Studying and stupefying are in the same sense akin: those who study are in the situation of people who have received a shock and are stupefied by what has struck them, unable to grasp it and, at the same time, powerless to leave hold. The scholar, that is, is always 'stupid'. But if, on the one hand, he is astonished and absorbed, if study is thus essentially a suffering and an undergoing [activity], the messianic legacy it contains drives him, on

the one hand, incessantly toward closure. This *festina lente*, this shuttling between bewilderment and lucidity, discovery and loss, agent and patient, is the rhythm of study.

(Agamben, 1995, p. 64)

The study seems to transcend infancy in the sense that being unable to speak is extended towards receiving 'a shock and [being] . . . stupefied' (Agamben, 1995, p. 64). To encounter new possibilities through studying opens one to learning something not known before, and being stupefied by it has some connection with recognising what one perhaps does not know. Put differently, through study, one becomes capable of speaking where clarity and discovery constantly emerge. The more one engages with a doctoral thesis, the more one begins to grasp it and is simultaneously powerless to leave hold (Agamben, 1995). In this sense, studying towards a doctorate becomes a sustained intellectual effort to put thought to paper with the recognition that one's writing remains in becoming. It is not as if one constantly grasps one's effort as one writes a text, but rather that one suffers an alteration every time one exerts oneself through writing. In this way, doctoral writing becomes one of whispering in the sense that one never completely knows what one has articulated through writing but is always willing to rethink and rearticulate one's initial thoughts. This kind of whispering Agamben (2007) refers to is known as studious play. So writing a doctorate based on whispering involves playfulness.

When students write doctorates, they also begin to set into motion new uses of the thoughts they put to paper. As they write their theses, they advance their thoughts on the subject matter in a ritualistic fashion through fixation and structuration – a matter of putting in place that which they are familiar with. Yet there comes a time when they also suspend the old uses of their thoughts to open the way for new enactments of such thoughts. Simply put, they find a different use for such thoughts, thus making their thoughts open to be played with (Agamben, 1995). They begin to disrupt their rituals in writing whereby thoughts and words are no longer fixed and structured but actually open to new dimensions and possibilities. As stated by Tyson Lewis (2013), their ritualised activities (of writing) take on a new use which sees their routine practices being suspended. I recall having encouraged students to just remain fixated on writing. But as their writing improved, students began to put more creative thoughts to paper. It is as if they suddenly unleashed more creative energy into their ritualised thoughts.

Without rushing through the thesis, a doctoral student embarks on studious play when she transcends her infancy and moves into the realm of studious play, where completion does not become an end in itself but where studying dominates her writing, always intent on seeing new dimensions in her work. When she is ready to submit her work for scrutiny by others, she temporarily

Whispering as studious and playful university education 17

suspends her study without the undertaking that her work has now reached finality. As Agamben (1995, p. 65) so poignantly reminds us:

> The end of study may never come – and, in this case, the work is stuck forever in the fragmentary or note stage.... But the latest, most exemplary embodiment of study in our culture is not the great philosopher or sainted doctor. It is rather the student... [who pursues her] study and returns to... inspiration.

To remain inspired is thus what studying towards a doctorate should be about so that students produce pieces of writing long after their doctorates have been examined. Inspirational thoughts often lead to creativity in writing. The idea of bringing doctoral writing into conversation with creativity is perhaps not new. Like art, writing is also considered a practice that has the potential to be creative. However, writing and creativity can enhance human actions vis-à-vis inspiration. Put differently, writing has the potential to be creative based on its interconnection with inspirational thoughts. Even now, while I am writing down thoughts that emanate from my mind, I recall having thought about creative writing earlier. After I thought about creativity in writing, I became more inspired to author something I had done previously.

Next, I examine how prominent whispering unfolded related to some doctoral students' work.

Whispering through doctoral education: some reminders of Nita, Marvin, Nancy, Tom, and Jerry

Nita was a typical example of a doctoral student who engaged with issues about women, cosmopolitanism, and democratic citizenship education. She began her infancy in the field of philosophy of education by putting into motion new and tentative understandings of cosmopolitanism, democracy, and citizenship in the realm of education. Through studious play, she considered how women would respond to the aforementioned notions in real-life experiences. As soon as she considered her work as completed, she was reminded that there was still more to do, so coming up with newer insights became synonymous with her work. The interesting aspect of Nita's writing is that she seldom considered her work as beyond reproach. Hence, she whispered as she endeavoured to revise her work coupled with immersing new insights into her writing. Yet sometimes she became too impetuous, ready to move on to the next thought. I often had to remind her to rethink moments in her writing and then develop a more creative proffering. Long after she completed her formal doctoral qualification, she still produces exemplary writing pieces. Thus, she commenced her academic career by whispering through a doctorate and wandered around coming up with more substantial pieces of writing as she began to consolidate her playfulness through writing. Nita's whispering seems to be an announcement of a restrained voice always willing to learn and to rearticulate her doctoral thoughts.

For several years Marvin painstakingly produced extensive pieces of writing and remained in a state of infancy as his writing, in many ways, was unable to respond to critical questions posed by his supervisor. Paradoxically speaking, it seemed he continuously wandered without giving himself opportunities to whisper. Yet, when he transcended the infancy stage, he became stupefied based on some of the claims he subsequently proffered, which his supervisor found persuasive enough. Through his deconstructive analysis of higher education in South Africa, he eventually managed to transcend his infancy and endeavoured to produce more credible pieces of writing. Marvin's endurance showed during doctoral writing is one way of confirming his whispering – that is, at all times, wanting to learn and to articulate himself more persuasively through his writing. Infancy and whispering brought to the fore in doctoral writing are characterised by three moments: a critical voice on the cusp of breaking through, a restrained voice, and a concerned voice in the sense that a student is on the verge of settling down but remains inspired to carry on writing. Unlike Nita, Marvin has not pursued the publications game, although they practically graduated simultaneously. I remember Marvin and Nita accompanying me to the annual philosophy of education conference at Oxford's New College, where they had to present their doctoral work (still in infant form at the time) at the meeting. This phenomenal academic experience invariably shaped the ensuing academic aspirations of these students. Their whispering took on new forms since their first exposure to such an academically rigorous conference. Like Nita, Nancy took on the project of revitalising an ethic of eco-justice education based on a religious text. She swiftly transcended her moment of infancy and quite confidently embarked on studious play based on producing laudable pieces of writing. Quite interestingly, Nancy argued how religio-cultural enunciations constitute eco-educational action. She still produces solid pieces of writing without occupying a formalised academic position. Even her interpretations of a religious text related to eco-justice proved somewhat understated due to her extended whispering period of writing.

Tom was a quintessential example of a student who joined the doctoral initiative with high levels of under-preparedness. But Tom's inability to interpret ideas resulted in my asking him to read and think for a whole year without writing a word on his doctorate. Of course, he was encouraged to make analytical summaries of his work and author such passages, but the focus should not have been on the writing itself. Focusing on managing racial integration in public schools, he began to write with more care and thoughtfulness after he spent some time reading and rereading volumes of texts on racial integration. Although his infancy in academic writing lasted longer than Jerry's, they managed to complete their doctoral writing almost simultaneously. Jerry's infant academic experience helped him scrutinise teachers' roles in philosophically assessing students' understanding of outcomes-based education in South Africa. Jerry's studious play allowed him to see new dimensions of assessment and schooling, which, disappointingly, he never really picked up on after completing his doctoral text. What was interesting about Jerry's experience is that he shared his intellectual space with Tom in many ways so that his passion for doctoral studies rubbed off on the latter. There existed an ethical friendship between them in the sense that they remained independent in their thoughts, but they were bound by a 'common strangeness' (Blanchot, 1971, p. 291).

These students always had the potential to speak: some spent more time during infancy, whereas others swiftly advanced into the realm of studious play. Nevertheless, their speaking contributed to viable doctoral writing acknowledged by some of the external examiners who had the privilege to comment on their work.

Summary

Doctoral writing fluctuates on a continuum between infancy and studious play. Students would not occupy the same position on the continuum as some spent longer in infancy than others. Yet having experienced moments of both infancy and studious play at different times, students managed to get their doctoral work done. For me, the doctoral thesis then becomes only a moment in time when the intellectual work of students is suspended to allow for the emergence of new openings and potentialities. A student never reaches closure as that would undermine the study that should remain interminable. In this sense, writing a doctorate remains a whispering of thought whereby it is recognised that there remains so much more to know and that an actual completion is never an option. Yet completion in the sense used earlier means that the document will be considered for submission for examination – which had been the case with doctoral students I supervised.

References

Agamben, G. (1995). *Idea of prose* (M. Sullivan & S. Whitsitt, Trans.). State University of New York Press.
Agamben, G. (2007). *Infancy and history: On the destruction of experience.* Verso.
Blanchot, M. (1971). *Friendship* (E. Rottenberg, Trans.). Stanford University Press.
CHE. (2022). *National review of South African doctoral qualifications 2020–2021: Doctoral degrees national report.* Author.
Jasinski, I. (2018). *Giorgio Agamben: Education without ends.* Springer.
Lewis, T. (2013). *On study: Giorgio Agamben and educational potentiality.* Routledge.

4 On utopianism and doctoral education

Introduction

If utopianism means perfection, then I have never encountered any doctoral thesis throughout my years in university education that has reached a stage of utopia. Doctoral thesis writing has always been challenging, exciting, and sometimes disappointing, especially when negative judgements are made about students' work or supervisors are blamed for not providing feedback on students' writing. It was never expected that doctoral studies would be easy, for that would undermine the rigour associated with such studies. Many institutions have only introduced mandatory agreements between supervisors and students because doctoral relations have not always been smooth and straightforward. This chapter examines if doctoral studies ought to be about attaining a state of utopia. Undeniably, completing a doctoral degree carries enormous external prestige and gain: the possibility of academic promotion, a recognition that someone has acquired a right of passage to undertake scholarly research, and even an acknowledgement that a person with a doctorate can provide expert advice on particular public matters. Be it as it may, a doctorate does hold certain material advantages to those who manage its successful completion. Yet a doctoral qualification also has an internal advantage in that those who successfully undertake such a journey should be capable of exercising an intellectual voice that enhances the expansion of knowledge claims in and about a particular subject matter. By this, it meant the capability of some to exercise their critical reason towards broadening intellectual truth claims about whatever subject matter they have pursued. Even so, having acquired both internal and external prowess in a particular subject matter through a doctorate has its limitations; otherwise the finality of argumentation would have been the outcome of doctoral completion. The central argument of this chapter is that the completion of a doctorate cannot be associated with perfectionism, as that condition in itself would be the end of higher education. Concomitantly, I also posit that doctoral education is about making some moral intervention into intellectual discourses to improve societal living and educational experiences. Doctoral studies, I argue, cannot be subjected to moral

DOI: 10.4324/9781032715872-4

blindness, especially about public matters that go against the advancement of moral action.

A doctorate and its limits of possibility

I once asked the renowned African philosopher Kwasi Wiredu about his doctoral studies, to which he replied that he did not complete such a formal qualification. Yet, undeniably, his intellectual contributions towards advancing African thought and practice throughout many years of scholarship have been immense. I inferred from Wiredu's response that (African) intellectualism does not necessarily depend on the achievement of some formal qualification but rather the responsiveness of academic argumentation to societal dystopias. Small wonder, Wiredu's seminal work involved cultivating a theory of African knowledge that could legitimately advance the continent's knowledge interests in resistance to coloniality and the exclusion of authentic and marginalised intellectual voices. However, his assertion that knowledge should have a liberatory intent does not imply that some blueprint for knowledge had to be produced in a utopian fashion that would guarantee Africa's liberation from colonial domination. Rather, as Wiredu (1992) purports, it would be difficult to advance the decolonial struggle when Africans' colonial mentality has not been critically and reconstructively self-evaluated and restored to a level of authentic consciousness. Here, Wiredu reminds us that decoloniality depends on developing a critical consciousness to resist oppression and exclusion in an ongoing way instead of producing a momentary template to counteract colonial subjugation. His commitment to a decolonial understanding of knowledge lies in cultivating a critical consciousness and not producing a formal qualification that might not be relevant to Africa's colonial predicament. Likewise, the focus of a decolonial mind ought to be on the continuous cultivation of a critical consciousness that would enable Africans to think differently and anew about their societal predicaments. For me, a critical conscientiousness begins with the autonomous self, whereby individuals think critically about their own work and the implications of such work for society at large. One cannot assume a critical consciousness when one fails to do so in relation to one's own pedagogical assumptions and claims. This also means considering assumptions that one's work is beyond criticism. It is to such a discussion that I now turn to.

Is the production of a 'perfect' doctorate possible?

There are at least three things wrong with utopianism: Firstly, utopianism implies that a doctorate is a completed text, and nothing can be extended about the thoughts embedded therein. Simply put, a utopian doctorate is an absolute text in which nothing can be altered about it. Such an idea of a doctorate would mark the end of higher education, where nothing new can be added to the ideas espoused in the text. The possibility to expand on ideas within the text becomes an impossibility because of its finality. Of course, completion means that the text has been examined and its arguments were found plausible and acceptable. However, plausibility and acceptability do not imply finality, as if the ideas in the text cannot be subjected to further scrutiny and/or elaboration. Secondly, a utopian doctorate is closed to new, rich, and even spectacular intellectual possibilities as it does not consider possible openness to other linguistic, cultural, artistic, and educational breakthroughs. Once the doctorate has been confirmed, its openness to otherness is resisted. By being closed to further examination and scrutiny, such a doctorate would prevent others from extending thoughts clarified in the text, which seems impossible. Thirdly, a doctorate considered utopian has procedurally fulfilled its course of argumentation and questioning. The very practice of argumentation is based on the understanding that humans see things differently as time elapses. And to prevent humans from doing so would do an injustice to doctoral work, which, in any case, is drawn to further elucidation and justification.

Now considering the above, the question can be asked: can texts ever be left unaltered, closed, and oppositional to further argumentation? My response is that any notion that turns its back on further reflection, as implied by unalteredness, closedness, and in opposition to extended argumentation, undermines the freedom of reflection associated with the intellectual discourses of a university. As Jacques Derrida (2004, p. 154) so aptly reminds us,

> [t]he time for reflection is also an other time; it is heterogeneous to what it reflects and perhaps gives time for what calls for and is called thinking. It is the time for an event about which one does not know whether or not, presenting itself within the university, it belongs to the history of the university.

Thus, closing the opportunity for further reflection on what utopianism does is an act of hostility to the university because it opposes and limits the essence of the university itself – that is, thinking. This is so because when a university is in a period of crisis or renewal, 'provocation to think brings together in the same instant the desire for memory and exposure to the future' (Derrida, 2004, p. 154). For this reason, the very notion of utopianism subverts the responsibility of the university to represent what is not yet (Derrida, 2004). What follows is that a utopian doctorate is hostile to the university's autonomy. It undermines the freedom of the university to exercise its professional rigour and competence, to postulate and be suspicious, and to play risks against another (Derrida, 2004). Put differently, utopianism prevents the university from taking a position that thinking inspires.

Is moral blindness an option in doctoral studies?

Many socio-political developments on the African continent seem to undermine moral integrity and peaceful living. At the time of writing, the ongoing conflict in Sudan between two war-mongering generals has left the country in ruins. Citizens cannot flee the conflict because they might be caught in the crossfire of bullets. The violence in the country occurs unabatedly, and even though a ceasefire has been called for, no party is prepared to cease its aggression. This is just one example of how warring factions in an African country undermine peaceful human co-existence, which leads me to assert that moral integrity is at stake as the fight for political power is violently exercised. If doctoral theses cannot be about speaking out against such unnecessary and unacceptable violence, then such theses invariably suffer from intolerable moral blindness. When high personal ambitions and self-interest of two generals can ignore the will of the people, then doctoral education cannot turn a blind eye to what is at hand. Similarly, other immoral incidences include human trafficking, child wars, women abuse and domestic violence, killings of those who expose corruption, and much more prevalent in Southern Africa. When doctoral students and supervisors turn a blind eye to moral dilemmas on the continent, theses often suffer from moral ineptitude. Consequently, I recognise the socio-political dilemma of violence on the African continent and invariably encourage my students to embark on doctoral studies that can address such moral dilemmas in African society and even in a university classroom. We guard against moral blindness, which would make our engagement with students unethical.

My point is that addressing moral blindness is far more urgent than the desire to achieve utopian doctoral studies. It seems more feasible to resist moral blindness than to be concerned about an objective utopian truth that is neither possible nor practical (Kavalnes, 2019). Next, I show why utopianism related to students' work becomes impossible.

Listening to Beth, Peter, and Ruby: on the limitlessness of freedom

Beth's doctoral investigation was inspired by a Freirean critical consciousness which she purported would enhance a praxis of hope in post-apartheid teacher education. For her, decoloniality was an oppositional act of freedom of reflection, according to which a combined notion of theory and practice in and about teacher education should be enhanced. Failing to reflect on ideas in one's thesis is tantamount to being remiss of a critical praxis that ought to guide decolonial initiatives in higher education. What makes Beth's thesis a moral inquiry is that she recognised a dilemma in teacher education in South Africa and endeavoured to respond to it with a Freirean notion of conscientisation. Equally, she envisaged that her doctoral work could contribute to emancipatory teacher education action. The point about reconceptualising teacher education in light of the notion of critical consciousness is a transformative act of change – that what was considered wrong and repressive in a newly established democratic society had to be changed morally as well.

Like Nellie's thesis analysed in Chapter 2, Peter also focused on the transformation of school governing bodies in post-apartheid South Africa. He posited that democratic school governing bodies have the potential to become morally responsive if organised along the lines of praxis, poiesis, and rhythm. For Peter, school governance ought to be transformative, considering the dominance of apartheid schooling in the past. In his view, it becomes a moral responsibility for school governors to ensure democratic citizenship education is enacted within governance structures. Whereas Nellie and Peter constructed educational transformation according to a Freirean notion of praxis, Ruby posited that higher education discourse ought to be constituted by an ethics of care. For her, an ethics of care is interrelated with reflective freedom that could enhance the inclusion of women in higher education discourses. Coupled with her argument for including women in educational discourses based on an ethics of care, she also argued for an amended version of *ubuntu* that relates to a non-coercive and non-repressive form of caring in and about educational relations. The authenticity of Ruby's doctoral work resided in her argument that *ubuntu* be expanded into the realm of caring, unlike previous understandings that the concept relates only to human dignity and interdependence.

The doctoral experiences of Beth, Peter, and Ruby can be articulated as decolonial actions constituted by critical consciousness, oppositional argumentation and resistance, and the freedom to reflect on higher educational discourses that remain open to reflective action that can deal adequately with societal dystopias. In many ways, their doctoral theses are examples of morally inspired work in that they are concerned with how humans can exercise their liberty and criticality in transformative practices. Put differently, by linking their doctoral work conceptually to a notion of critical praxis, their work took an unexpected decolonial turn.

Summary

I have argued that associating doctoral education at a university with utopianism is an impossibility not worth embarking on. This association would curb the university from exercising its academic responsibility to think. Thinking is synonymous with pursuing reflections – wondering, wandering, and whispering – through which a university remains open to the possibility of being altered and playing risks against another so necessary for a future yet to come. In the latter context, doctoral theses will remain open texts only to be considered as completed in the context of examination-ready writing pieces.

In the main, as far as doctoral theses are concerned, utopianism is not commensurate with a doctoral journey. Utopianism seems to promote the possibility that doctoral thesis writing is infallible. On the contrary, acts of freedom and reflection are intended to retain the openness associated with doctoral texts, thus attesting to their moral and epistemological fallibility. In the same way, critical consciousness requires students to be vigilant and alert to the transformative potential of their work, which, in any case, seems to negate any utopian obsession with doctoral work. What seems more relevant is the possibility that doctoral work can be more morally responsive than any form of utopianism that might never exist.

References

Derrida, J. (2004). *Eyes of the university: Right to philosophy 2* (J. Plug et al., Trans.). Stanford University Press.
Kavalnes, Ø. (2019). *Moral reasoning at work*. Palgrave Macmillan.
Wiredu, K. (1992). Problems in Africa's self-definition in the contemporary world. In K. Wiredu & K. Gyekye (Eds.), *Person and community. The council for research in values and philosophy* (pp. 40–59). The Council for Research in Values and Philosophy.

5 Towards ethical pedagogical encounters between supervisors and students

Introduction

In previous chapters, I have argued why wondering, wandering, and whispering should be associated with a university, specifically doctoral education. I now examine why these moral acts of university life should be connected with doctoral supervision. I specifically focus on doctoral education as an ethical encounter between supervisors and students. That is, when pedagogical encounters between supervisors and students are pursued, the likelihood that such encounters would remain ethical depends on how initiation, lucidity, and rhythm are enacted in morally defensible ways. Put differently, to take the initiative, be clear, and be rhythmic relate to the moral competence that supervisors and students possess that would enable them to enhance pedagogical encounters. Such a view finds resonance in the seminal thoughts of Elina Kuusisto and Kirsi Tirri (2013), for whom active democratic citizens must be ethically (morally) sensitive in their educational encounters.

On the necessity of whispering, wondering, and wandering during doctoral supervision: cultivating moral virtues of doctoral encounters

It would be unbecoming of me to intimate that doing doctoral studies begins with a specific action separate from supervisors and students. Rather, I think of doctoral education as an autonomous and iterative encounter between a supervisor and a student. Doctoral education cannot unfold without students having a desire and willingness to pursue such advanced studies. Similarly, supervisors should be keen on supporting doctoral education, perhaps as part of an institution's research agenda. I now examine why I consider doctoral education intellectually and morally worthwhile to consider.

Firstly, based on my academic experiences over many years, I invitingly propose that students ought to embark on whispering when they initiate their doctoral pursuits. Through whispering, one immediately assumes a humble demeanour when one begins with a doctorate. To be humble implies that one recognises that there is so much to gain during this intellectual and moral journey – an intellectual path of insights, reflections, and pursuits and a moral path of coming up with something that can be justified ethically. One also appreciates that one will not get it right instantly, but by browsing through the literature pertaining to one's field of inquiry, one identifies the positions and arguments of others as they pronounce their claims of educational matters that concern their inquiries. So to whisper means to make tentative analyses of what one reads and understands and concomitantly formulate their arguments in writing – of course, in typing too! When one engages with others' views, one gets some understanding of the field or discipline one examines. As for a supervisor, it seems her role is to encourage students to come up with their understandings with which she (the supervisor) engages. This would be a recognition of the autonomy of students whose analyses of texts a supervisor arduously engages with. It can also be that a student is supervised by a group of scholars contributing to doctoral education. A supervisor does not just tell students what to do but summons them to use their equal intelligence to come to speech (and writing). In this way, supervision becomes an act of provocation. Students are invited to think for themselves and put their initial thoughts in writing. It could be that supervisors refer students to some books and summon them to come up with their reading of the books. For instance, I am thinking of summoning my students to books on democratic citizenship education. They are required to read and analyse at least three books and then to share with us (students and I) their individual interpretations of the main claims about democratic citizenship education they have come across in the books. And as they engage the literature, they whisper with authority and a lack thereof. It is not always that students analyse texts in commanding ways. Some students are hesitant to get it wrong. But as they continue with their analyses, they become more adept at doing so to the extent that they come to understand with more authority. It is not that we insist students gain some mastery of the texts. Mastery is an impossibility because what one interprets is how one perceives an author's writing. It might not have been what the author intended. But by analysing someone else's views, one invariably comes up with an individualised notion of what an author intended. In this way, one derives some subjective understanding of the author's position. However, I require students to share their understanding with us about the books they were asked to comment on.

For students, whispering is a matter of gaining confidence in their analyses and not mastery – the latter will always remain an impossibility and rightly so. The point I am making is that supervisors should encourage students to read in their fields of inquiry by consulting the most pertinent journal articles and books about their own investigations. They must initiate themselves and be initiated further into the central debates and arguments that constitute their fields of inquiry. It does not make sense to assume that one will understand one's field of investigation without referring to literature that advances ideas pertaining to one's studies. Doctoral education does not unfold in a vacuum, and there will always be something that one might not have considered. In this way, initiation becomes a significant action to embark on. And it invariably helps doctoral pursuits when supervisors offer readings students can acquaint themselves with as they pursue their intellectual and moral journeys. Of course, some institutions implement doctoral programmes to initiate students into specific fields of inquiry. I might not necessarily concur with such initiatives because students should show that they are conscientious about undergoing alterity themselves based on taking their own initiatives. If too much is being done and organised for students, they tend to become less authoritative in doing their doctorates. To always rely on others to do things for oneself takes away from one's autonomy to initiate things – that is, what doctoral studies earnestly require. For this reason, I encourage students to whisper and take small steps to pursue their studies.

Secondly, doctoral thesis writing, like any thesis for that matter, must be lucid, perspicuous, and a discourse that raises doubt. To author a cogent and unambiguous text is necessary for defence of the arguments one proffers, on the one hand. Academic writing does not have to be muddled and incoherent, for that would obscure meanings. Even the use of flowery language can be discouraging for one's readers. I recall some supervisors who insisted on textual clarity and coherence devoid of a language that adumbrated meanings. On the other hand, the point about raising doubts in one's doctoral work is meant to reconsider and rearticulate one's thoughts in writing. Raising doubts – a matter of being sceptical – allows one to open one's writing to multivarious possibilities in the sense that one would be obliged to relook at one's claims about educational matters. Only then, the act of gracefully and distinctively authoring one's text becomes highly likely. Graceful writing is a form of elegance according to which words, phrases, sentences, and paragraphs are introduced in an unobtrusive manner that provokes the interests of one's readers. In this way, wonderment would be procured. Wonder is considered an experience of puzzlement and mystification (Schinkel, 2020). It assumes a form of inquisitiveness in solving one's puzzlement through understanding and explanation (Schinkel, 2020). It can also be aesthetic, joyful, unsettling, and close to awe (Schinkel, 2020). Often students during their initiation phase are confounded by ideas they have to put into writing and experience moments of disquietude as they endeavour to construct their arguments. And, when they get it right, they experience an unfettered joyfulness. Their moments of disquietude and unfettered joy invariably contribute to an easing of doubt in their work. Yet the presence of doubt allows them to rethink and rearticulate meanings that constitute their doctoral work.

Thirdly, as a proponent of rhythmic action – suspension and advancement – it seems prudent to supervise doctoral students in such a manner. When students author their texts, there comes a time when they experience what is commonly known as mental blocks. Some students' minds simply drift towards other things, such as cleaning, cooking, and exercising, without retaining their focus on the task at hand. Their drifting experiences cause them to become directionless, often not knowing where the next sentence will come from. It is then that students should be interrupted in their writing to stimulate them towards some focus, such as challenging them about this or that matter in their theses. Such a momentary interruption would hopefully result in a temporary suspension of their writing to again pick up where they left off – that is, suspending their writing to advance again later. This kind of rhythmic action provokes them to suspend their writing momentarily only to resume writing after a short while, which could be to rethink their doctoral project. Many of the students supervised throughout my career experienced moments of suspension and advancement – that is, they held back on their writing only to rekindle their interest in their work and then to make strides towards its actualisation. Yet, when these students actualised their writing again, they would be reminded that what they now came up with should be considered a potential step in the appropriate direction. My insistence that potentiality should remain part of their writing is to remind them that there remains much to know and learn about.

Mary, Tarryn, and Janet: from initiation to rhythm

Initiation and infancy, lucidity and doubt, and suspension and resumption are moments students experience in their doctoral writing. In this way, it can be argued that their writing is a form of ethical action constituted by moral instances of initiation, doubt, and rhythm. Doctoral writing seems to be both a forward-looking and backwards-looking activity based on interruptions in writing that can boost pedagogical encounters among supervisors and students. Interruptions are meant to make students rethink their claims and writing, not just criticism they must endure. Mary, Tarryn, and Janet were all initiated into doctoral writing as infants with much to realise in pursuing a doctorate. Mary was initiated into a discourse of democratic citizenship education in some sceptical way because she was not entirely convinced that higher education discourse in her native country ought to be looked at commensurate with such a political and moral discourse. She eventually suspended her writing after first having to have made sense of the concept in relation to higher pedagogy before she resumed again in a coherent and plausible way. What interests me about Mary is her admission and recognition that her thoughts about democratic citizenship education needed to be augmented and thus she got stuck into readings about the discourse. She realised that she would not be able to make sense of a reconsidered notion of higher education if she did not critically analyse and brush up on her thoughts about democratic citizenship education. Often when I visited Mary in the office dedicated to students, she would stare at the clippings on the wall in her way to make sense of the authors' theoretical understandings of democratic citizenship education.

Tarryn was by far the best writer in her group and succeeded in initiating herself into a discourse of critical agency coupled with a consideration of its implications for South African teacher education. Having been a teacher in the United States for almost a decade, her critical reflections on her teaching in Black schools gave her an intellectual and moral edge over her fellow students in critical race theory. Her coherence and argumentation were so impeccable that some of her examiners raised unnecessary doubts about the authenticity of her writing at a time when AI ChatGPT was not yet around. This situation was eventually resolved when she pointed out that scepticism is a necessary form of inquiry which led her to defend her thesis more persuasively to her examiners during the mandatory viva voce. During the viva voce, she attentively listened to examiners' queries and stood back before she responded so competently to the scepticism that surrounded her writing. What I have learned about Tarryn is that doing a doctorate also requires some moral composure in the face of suspicion and doubt about one's work. Moral composure is connected to providing a justification for the arguments one articulates and pointing out the goodness in such arguments for societal living. And this Tarryn seemed to have done ably in the context of teacher education in South Africa. The scepticism surrounding her doctoral work emanated from an article she used as a Turnitin example at the institution where she previously assisted the editor of a prominent academic journal. Some editorial committees in South Africa use the Turnitin programme to test the similarity of academic work. Considering that Tarryn already tested an article for consideration as a case study for the journal she assisted with, her doctoral work that was subsequently tested for similarity scored high on the similarity index because it compared with her unpublished article used in a similarity test. Nevertheless, this matter was dealt with, and Tarryn's performance during the viva voce exonerated her from the suspicion of plagiarism.

Like Mary, Janet was also initiated into a discourse of democratic citizenship education which she contended could significantly influence a discourse of higher education. She also pointed out the political and moral ramifications of such a discourse for higher education discourse in her native country. Only after being questioned about the authenticity of her arguments did she step back and respond eloquently to the concerns of at least two examiners during her viva voce. Her competence and familiarity with the subject matter that she acquired during her initiation phase helped her convince others of her argument. What interests me about Janet's responses to her examiners is how she invoked arguments about decolonisation to point out how dominant discourses seem pervasive in the literature and how her examiners could have used some of such discourses to counter her arguments.

Summary

I have made a case for wondering, wandering, and whispering as ethical virtues of doctoral supervision. Without the desire to speak tentatively, persuasively, gracefully, sceptically, and rhythmically – all moral instances of doctoral education – there is no point in doctoral supervision. What I have argued for in this chapter is in defence of a three-phased approach to doctoral writing: firstly, an initiation phase whereby students labour to articulate speech based on what they have read, thought about, and interpreted; secondly, an experience of doubt whereby they questioned their own assumptions about their doctoral work as well as their writing; and thirdly, an enactment of rhythmic action whereby they encountered moments of suspension only to resume again at a later stage in their doctoral pursuits. The processes of initiation, raising doubt, and enacting rhythm occur in an intertwined way in the actualisation of the doctorate so that the latter remains in potentiality.

References

Kuusisto, E., & Tirri, K. (2013). Teachers' moral competence in pedagogical encounters. In W. Veugelers (Ed.), *Education for democratic intercultural citizenship* (pp. 81–106). Brill.

Schinkel, A. (Ed.). (2020). *Wonder, education, and human flourishing: Theoretical, empirical and practical perspectives.* VU University Press.

6 Doctoral supervision and the enactment of democratic citizenship education

Introduction

In the previous chapter, I have shown how notions of democratic citizenship education were used by some students to actualise their doctoral writing. In this chapter, I specifically focus on the notion of democratic citizenship education and how it relates to doctoral supervision. Intertwining notions of democratic citizenship education with doctoral supervision is an edifying and radical idea. Its edification is connected to the educational potential of both practices – that is, democratic citizenship education and doctoral supervision, on the one hand. On the other hand, its radicalism is linked to its revolutionary potential. More succinctly, democratic citizenship education or, as Wiel Veugelers (2019) refers to it, democratic and intercultural citizenship education can enhance human flourishing because diverse people come together to cooperate and deliberate about living a good life. In this way, edification and radicalism are necessary to cultivate a sustainable, dynamic, and future-oriented society (Veugelers, 2019). In this chapter, firstly, I analyse the notion of democratic citizenship education; secondly, I show why democratic citizenship education and doctoral supervision are interdependent practices; and thirdly, I argue why combining these practices cultivates a notion of intellectual activism to corroborate their moral radicalism.

Rethinking democratic citizenship education

To begin with, the notion of education is constituted by an individual and communitarian dimension. As an individual action, education is considered the pursuit of competencies and skills by individual persons. In other words, when individuals exercise their capacities to enact intellectual enterprises, they are considered to engage in education. For instance, when persons embark on reading philosophy of higher education, they are said to engage educationally. Inasmuch as such a view has been dominant over many decades, this is not the view of education I consider mutually intertwined with democratic citizenship. Rather, the view of education as an encounter seems

DOI: 10.4324/9781032715872-6

more apposite for elucidating education coupled with a notion of democratic citizenship. Hence, I rely on the seminal thoughts of Jane R. Martin (2013), who purports that education is an encounter between the individual self and other selves in the process of yoking together different cultures. When persons of different cultures associate, they form an encounter based on their engagement with one another's thoughts and practices. In this way, education as an encounter is a communitarian action. In communitarian practices, people act democratically, inclusively, and critically as they engage one another in sociopolitical and moral action (Veugelers, 2019).

Notions of democracy and citizenship provide encounters with a sociopolitical and moral impetus. Veugelers and De Groot (2019) cogently accentuate some of the transitions democratic citizenship education has undergone: from a rights and responsibilities discourse in the 1960s; to societally reproductive action in the 1970s; to critical and transformative pedagogical action in the 1980s; to psychological and philosophical discourses in the 1990s; and since the 2000s, to post-colonial and indigenous discourses. Democratic citizenship is premised on three assumptions: every citizen has an equal opportunity to engage in a discourse; citizens are free to engage, thus maximising its egalitarianism; and citizens have to contend with pervasive inequalities at the level of the social, economic, and political aspects of life (Anagnostopoulos & Santas, 2018). If one thinks about democratic citizenship in relation to doctoral supervision, then supervisors and students become co-citizens in the discourse of supervision. That is, supervisors and students are equal participants in the supervisory process as they have equal opportunities to contribute to the development of the thesis. Students author their texts, and supervisors equally scrutinise and interpret the texts. Supervisors are free to comment on students' writing to which students are at liberty to respond, albeit in agreement and dissensus. Although supervisors and students engage freely and equally, doctoral supervision unfolds unequally based on the advice students gain from their supervisors; the unequal levels of knowledge of both participants and the prescriptive guidelines students have to adhere to in writing their theses. The point is that looking at doctoral supervision as a democratic citizenry experience implies that supervisors and students engage as equals and free participants in the pursuit of producing theses. It is not as if supervisors should only tell students what to do. Rather, iterative engagement must unfold between a supervisor and a student (verbally or in writing) to produce a more authentic doctoral text. Equally, students rely on supervisors to provide advice and act autonomously to ensure that doctoral texts are lucid, rigorous, and plausible. Next, we examine the notion of a doctoral encounter.

Doctoral supervision as an educational encounter

Undoubtedly, doctoral supervision involves humans – supervisors and students – which makes it an educational experience. An educational experience is cultivated by supervisors and students who engage with one another. This implies students enact their reading, talking, and writing as legitimate participants in an educational experience. Supervisors, in turn, read and advise students on the plausibility of their doctoral work or not. In this way, supervisors equally engage with students. Considering that engagement constitutes an educational experience and encounters are also underscored by forms of engagement, it is not untenable to speak about educational experiences as encounters. In this way, doctoral supervision is tantamount to an encounter between a supervisor and her students. Doctoral encounters occur based on students and supervisors en-gaging with one another. Etymologically speaking, the prefix 'en' implies that people do things together or in a combined way, whereas 'gaging' derives from gauge, which means to work out or determine. So an encounter implies that people do things together, intending to work out. That is, doctoral students and supervisors engage in doctoral education with the aim to ascertain or find out what has been done.

The question arises: What do supervisors do when they engage with students in educational encounters? Firstly, students produce texts about their doctoral work, which they present (make known) to supervisors. Put differently, their texts represent the doctoral work they pursue. With relative autonomy, supervisors reflect on the work students produce. They insert their thinking into students' theses. For some years, I had a doctoral student who did not submit any substantive work to me for consideration, which meant that this occurrence would hardly count as an encounter. Secondly, when supervisors comment on students' work, they provoke students to think more about their theses and come up with future possibilities. Supervisors thus assume a responsibility to advise students to look beyond what they do not have, and as Jacques Derrida (2004, p. 155) avers, 'what is not yet'. Thirdly, students' potentialities are evoked to take risks and to play off risks against one another to produce more substantive thought pieces in their doctoral work. It seems as if doctoral supervision is aimed at summoning students to come to writing without hesitancy and the possibility that they might be wrong. In this way, an educational encounter is a form of learning with doubt and mistakes with the possibility that texts can be tweaked and refined.

Cultivating intellectual and moral activism through doctoral studies

Intellectual and moral activism is a term coined by Patricia Hill Collins (2013) that denotes alternative analyses of social injustices, particularly disrupting existing power relations in social institutions. At least three issues emerge from Collins's idea of intellectual and moral activism: Firstly, an intellectual and moral activist does alternative analyses of social injustices. Here, I specifically think of theses about the educational implications of migration in the Global South, the resistance to patriarchal practices and gender-based violence in African communities, and the lack of deliberative engagement among university teachers and students in attempts to decolonise university practices in Africa. For example, deliberative engagements among teachers and students have mostly been explained in light of teachers' autonomy. However, following an alternative analysis of such engagements, one can look at deliberation in the context of how students respond to ensure their continued inclusion in an encounter. Students exercise their equal intelligence in encounters with teachers based on exercising their speech (Rancière, 2011).

Secondly, intellectual and moral activism aims to subvert hegemonic discourses based on claims of iterative action through which humans engage in transformative action. I specifically consider the production of theses that uses iterative argumentation to oppose dominant educational discourses that exclude and marginalise human action. The point is that intellectual and moral activism seems to resist action that restricts human engagement. Teachers and students engage iteratively when they equally exercise their legitimate right to speech acts without being constrained to do so.

Thirdly, humans are urged to exercise their capacities for reasonable speech to be intellectually and morally active. This means that humans must produce texts that are open to otherness in what is not yet. In this regard, the production of theses that accentuates actions such as rethinking, reconsidering, reconceptualising, reimagining, and deconstructing is grounded in assumptions that educational matters can be different in a way that responds to major analytical and pragmatic concerns about issues of democracy, citizenship, cosmopolitanism, equality, equity, and transformation vis-à-vis higher educational matters.

Doctoral work that cultivates intellectual and moral activism in reference to Sandy, Moody, and Manny

The doctoral works of Sandy, Moody, and Manny are typical examples of students who endeavoured to focus on intellectual and moral activism in their theses. Sandy philosophically analysed curriculum policy and student access into the industry to respond to the moral concern that higher education produces students inadequately prepared for the world of work. In this way, her work offered a pragmatic intellectual and moral response to the dilemma of demand and supply for industry in her native country. What is interesting about Sandy's work is that students' lack of access to universities is considered an intellectual and moral dilemma: as an intellectual predicament, some students are deprived of gaining access to universities due to material constraints of funding, institutional capacity, and the unavailability of supervisors, and, as a moral predicament, students would not be provided with an opportunity to produce higher work related to responding to moral crises on the continent.

Moody averred that higher education quality assurance ought to be rethought vis-à-vis its implications for university teaching and learning. Her work could be regarded as providing an alternative analysis of quality assurance and its implications for higher pedagogy in Southern Africa. Whereas a lack of quality assurance undermines intellectual integrity, it minimises the moral veracity that should be associated with doctoral work relevant to societies in need. Unlike Sandy and Moody, Manny provided an alternative analysis of democratic citizenship education in primary school education as a pragmatic and moral way to address concerns about undemocratic schooling practices. The point is that Manny's doctoral work accentuated a lack of intellectual activism in educational discourses and a dearth of work dealing with societal moral development.

Thus, Sandy, Moody, and Manny were all concerned with the relevance of their doctoral work to resisting pedagogical and moral injustices (an instance of societal injustices) in educational institutions. And this they all tackled by resisting immoral and unintellectual action that seemingly constrains human engagement in society, whether in schools or universities.

Summary

In this chapter, I have argued for a notion of doctoral supervision open to cultivating democratic citizenship in (higher) education. When doctoral supervision is commensurate with the cultivation of democratic citizenship education, the chances are more likely that (higher) education would be transformed intellectually, politically, and morally – that is, ethically. In this regard, Gert Biesta (2014, p. 7) opines that democratic citizenship education 'should be understood as a process of transformation'. But then, alternative analyses of pedagogical injustices, resisting actions that seemingly constrain human encounters, and concerns with pragmatic and moral responsiveness ought to constitute doctoral work.

References

Anagnostopoulos, G., & Santas, G. (Eds.). (2018). *Democracy, justice, and quality in ancient Greece: Historical and philosophical perspectives*. Springer.

Biesta, G. (2014). Learning in public spaces: Civic learning for the twenty-first century. In G. Biesta, M. De Bie, & D. Wildemeersch (Eds.), *Civic learning, democratic citizenship and the public sphere* (pp. 1–14). Springer.

Collins, P. H. (2013). Truth-telling and intellectual activism. *Contexts, 12*(1), 36–39.

Derrida, J. (2004). *Eyes of the university: Right to philosophy 2* (J. Plug et al., Trans.). Stanford University Press.

Martin, J. R. (2013). *Education reconfigured: Culture, encounter, and change*. Routledge.

Rancière, J. (2011). The thinking of dissensus: Politics and aesthetics. In P. Bowman & R. Stamp (Eds.), *Reading Rancière: Critical dissensus* (pp. 1–17). Continuum.
Veugelers, W., & De Groot, I. (2019). Theory and practice of citizenship education. In W. Veugelers (Ed.), *Education for democratic intercultural citizenship* (pp. 14–41). Brill.

7 Doctoral education and the enactment of cosmopolitan justice

Introduction

To associate doctoral education with cosmopolitan justice is a recognition that such a form of education has some intellectual, socio-political, and moral purpose. This is so on account of two issues. First is cosmopolitanism which reveres reasoned intellectualism as the basis of all human action; secondly, all humans should be held accountable to moral standards of equal respect (Nussbaum, 2010). Likewise, cosmopolitan justice involves cultivating human forms of living based on intercultural and just forms of exchange among pluralist communities (Todd, 2010). Gauging from the Council on Higher Education's (CHE) review of doctoral education in South Africa, there seems to be a dearth of theses addressing issues of cosmopolitan justice in Southern Africa (CHE, 2022). I specifically refer to theses that address issues of migration, inhospitality, and exclusion of humans who seek refuge in neighbouring countries after having endured war and terror in their home countries. In this chapter, I analyse a notion of cosmopolitan justice and make a case for why doctoral theses should not be oblivious to the need for an education that addresses a defensible form of cosmopolitanism.

What constitutes cosmopolitan justice? And what should be its impact on doctoral supervision?

Following the seminal thoughts of Jacques Derrida (2010), cosmopolitan justice involves three practices: Firstly, it refers to the right of immunity and hospitality accorded to people who have been censored, terrorised, persecuted, and enslaved (Derrida, 2010, p. 5). Here, I specifically think of many African immigrants who are forced to flee their home countries due to the threat of incarceration and death. Secondly, cosmopolitan justice recognises the rights of migrants to temporary residence in foreign countries (Derrida, 2010). Thirdly, cosmopolitan justice offers conditional hospitality to migrants, which is 'provisional upon the cultivation of newly established democratic communities that can live peacefully and responsibly together' (Derrida, 2010, p. 12).

My interest is in establishing democratic communities that can live peacefully and responsibly. For such communities to flourish, they should be open to others, and their differences are based on '[an] openness to debate and interaction, respect for the elementary traditions and procedures that make group life possible, and a willingness to restrain and mitigate sectarian enmities' (Waldron, 2003, p. 43). By implication, the cultivation of democratic communities depends on people's willingness to engage one another iteratively and to recognise one another's differences in an atmosphere of responsible action.

If one considers this notion of cosmopolitanism related to doctoral supervision, then supervisors and students should remain open to debate and interaction. This means that opportunities must be created for doctoral students to present some of their ideas in their theses and to engage with others about the authenticity or not of their work. In this way, seminars become spaces for disputes in and about doctoral work. The point is that seminars become epistemological gateways for elucidations in and about knowledge expositions. Doctoral work that is not exposed to debate and interaction has little chance of becoming rigorous pieces of writing where substantiation and erudition are at stake. The procedure of iteration whereby students and supervisors could engage in a constant to-and-fro of idea formation should become a much-needed space for intellectual controversy. There is no point in doing doctoral work that is not ever subjected to contention and disputation as if everything a student writes should be uncritically accepted as valid and substantial. What is the point of doing a doctorate that is unvindicable? It is through vulnerability that thoughts become more tenable and judicious. It would be catastrophic to know that doctoral work has never been exposed to authentic scrutiny by others. Yet, in its exposure to iteration, there is always the opportunity for students to become less reliant on supervisors as they continue to rearticulate their writing in the presence of others. In turn, supervisors restrain themselves from becoming too instructive about what students conjure up and present as credible written pieces. Here, reference to pieces of writing is connected to the idea that thesis writing is a matter of putting together thoughts in much the same way one would bring together pieces of a puzzle. At times, doctoral writing is confounding, and at other times, it is comprehensible in much the same way rhythm unfolds. The notion of rhythm is connected to holding back on one's judgement to allow students to articulate themselves freely without being constrained by the premature judgements of supervisors. Only when students have said what they wanted to say can supervisors interrupt their writing by commenting constructively on their work. We do not think it is helpful for supervisors to dismiss students' work, for that kind of discouragement would be quite disheartening, especially when one considers students have put some effort into their writing. Also, doctoral writing cannot be without paradoxes, which would render writing defenceless. There is no need for supervisors to over-exuberantly orchestrate how theses should unfold. That would undermine doctoral students' autonomy as genuine authors in becoming. In fact, writing a doctoral thesis should not be about achieving predetermined outcomes, for that would subvert the unexpected, improbable, and incalculable associated with a thesis at this level. Surely what should emerge should not have been stated in advance, for that would nullify the research that would have ensued. Supervisors of doctoral work have to be willing to restrain and mitigate speech so that students can compose their writing as they prefer. The point is that treating students' work justly implies that supervisors must recognise their students' writing styles and not unilaterally impose their writing prowesses on students.

Cosmopolitan justice in relation to the work of Harry, Jenny, and Zara

Next, I show how cosmopolitan justice unfolded in the context of three students' work. Harry submitted his doctoral thesis in the Afrikaans parlance – that is, his home language and the language spoken by a section of the minority white and coloured communities in South Africa. Yet his arguments in defence of inclusive democratic citizenship education as a response to indiscipline and instances of violence in some South African schools made sense. For Harry, no form of justice should be considered relevant for education if it cannot be attentive to all who engage with their differences and otherness in such encounters. This response might seem obvious; however, considering that educational relations in post-apartheid South Africa are supposedly meant to be democratic, such relations seem to succumb to exclusion and marginalisation. And, for Harry to make the argument in his doctoral thesis is a reminder of the moral commitment he seems to advance in and through his studies. As aptly reminded by David T. Hansen (2011, p. 90), cosmopolitan doctoral education 'embodies an attempt to fuse the moral and the ethical – that is to say, to merge the cultivation of the self (ethics) in its humane relation with others and the world (the moral)'.

Similarly, Jenny's doctoral thesis was written and submitted in her second language, English, with which she might not always have felt as confident as she would be in her mother tongue, Afrikaans. And her doctoral thesis was persuasive enough as she showed how university accounting education requires curricula that address cultivating socially responsible citizens. Jenny took issue with accounting education in South Africa, which she considered exclusive and anti-cosmopolitan because it failed to address a moral imperative of higher education transformation in the country. In this way, cosmopolitan injustice seemed to be a significant argument in her thesis. In the main, her contention was that unless accounting education can engender responsible citizens, such studies would not contribute significantly to the politico-moral purposes of doctoral education.

Zara, who was very adept at writing in the English language, showed not only a critical stance on doctoral thesis writing can improve one's articulation of arguments and claims but also how teacher education in South Africa could benefit from the integration of critical skills into university (science education) curricula. Although science education curricula should address issues of a lack of criticality and unreasonableness, she argued that university science education curricula do not always teach students critical thinking competencies and skills to deal with their seemingly non-transformative curricula.

What stands out in these theses is the ability of students to articulate their arguments in their preferred languages without the constraints of a language that might have inhibited their doctoral work. Of course, thesis writing has to be articulated in a language accessible to readers, especially supervisors and examiners. But when the arguments proffered are not persuasive enough, then such theses do not honour the rigorous work of doctoral students. Unless doctoral theses were to take up issues pertaining to a lack of critical thinking skills, university education in the country would fail in its attempt to be transformative in a democratic and cosmopolitan way. Consequently, doctoral education has an intellectual and socio-political purpose and needs to respond morally to many undesirable practices that have found their way into university education.

Summary

Doctoral work should be considered as writing in becoming where sublimity cannot be an option. Writing of theses should invariably be subjected to the art of debate and interaction, iteration, and a willingness of supervisors to restrain and mitigate excessive involvement in the doctorate itself. Only then would the possibility of producing a lucid, coherent, and judicious text remain in becoming. Likewise, supervisors cannot coerce students to write theses in a style they are most familiar with, for that would detract from the richness of the doctoral work couched in students' language. Finally, doctoral supervision should involve cultivating cosmopolitan justice so that students respond ethically to some of the moral concerns about education in their communities and engage iteratively and responsibly with their supervisors in recognition of differences and otherness in and about thesis writing. And, when doctoral theses do not respond to moral dilemmas on the African continent, such works would not do justice to several crises that arise.

References

CHE. (2022). *National review of South African doctoral qualifications 2020–2021: Doctoral degrees national report*. Author.

Derrida, J. (2010). *On cosmopolitanism and forgiveness* (M. Dooley & M. Hughes, Trans.). Routledge.

Hansen, D. T. (2011). *The teacher and the world: A study of cosmopolitanism as education*. Routledge.

Nussbaum, M. C. (2010). Kant and cosmopolitanism. In G. Wallace-Brown & D. Held (Eds.), *The cosmopolitan reader* (pp. 27–44). Policy Press.

Todd, S. (2010). Living in a dissonant world: Toward an agonistic cosmopolitics for education. *Studies in Philosophy and Education, 29*(1), 213–228.

Waldron, J. (2003). Teaching cosmopolitan rights. In K. McDonough & W. Feinberg (Eds.), *Citizenship and education in liberal-democratic societies* (pp. 23–55). Oxford University Press.

8 Doctoral supervision and the notion of critique

Introduction

Undeniably, universities have always been associated with the notion of critique or a form of thinking (Waghid & Davids, 2020). Any attempt to delink universities from critique would subvert what a university stands for. Critique is a form of thinking that attests to human understanding and knowing. It gives universities the intellectual space to open up to the others (Biesta, 2009). Critique is also that form of thinking that resists enslavement, subjugation, and control. Consequently, it is an act of empowerment whereby those who embark on critique consider themselves liberators from hegemonic discourses. If thinking cannot be free and unconstrained, there is no point in thinking at all. In this chapter, I re-examine a notion of critique and consider its implications for doctoral supervision. The point of this chapter is to show how difficult it is for university education to abandon critique and that it would implicate any doctoral study that runs the risk of subverting critique.

On critique as thinking

Since the 19th century, when Wilhelm von Humboldt founded an institution in Germany where autonomous scholars pursued their fields of inquiry, critique has always been associated with university education. More recently, Michel Foucault (1988) explains critique as sudden upheavals of thought according to which university teachers and students make sense of educational matters that concern them. And, in their attempts to infer meanings about such matters, they reflect freely or autonomously as they endeavour to address educational matters. When such matters are controversial, they are equally adept at providing insights through their interrogations. In this way, teachers and students neither totally accept elucidations nor reject in their entirety interpretations about education. As Foucault (1988) posits, they remain in a state of discomfort and defiance about educational matters. The latter recognises that uncritical agreement and wholesome disagreement are not options to consider through critique. Concerning doctoral supervision, supervisors should substantiate their discomfort with

DOI: 10.4324/9781032715872-8

students' work and, at the same time, not in its entirety, dismiss their work as irrelevant and baseless. Supervisors need to take a keen interest in the arguments proffered by students and should not treat students' work with disdain as if their (students') writing cannot be salvaged. Likewise, it would be unwise for students to outright reject supervisors' comments about their work, for that would deprive them of rethinking some of their writing and making adjustments – responding to disagreement. In this regard, Masek and Alias (2020) posit that significant doctoral supervision depends greatly on conceptual clarification – that is, expositions of claims subjected to critique. Doctoral theses that have not been subjected to critique suffer the loss of a genuine rigour of engagement.

Secondly, critique as dissensus implies that one puts into question what one thinks is wrong with what is presented. What is wrong can be both intellectually and morally so. It is intellectually inappropriate or wrong to assume that paradigms of thinking do not influence human action. When humans think, they do so based on their lifeworlds or frameworks of thinking that influence their ways of seeing events in the world. Similarly, it seems morally wrong to suggest that excommunicating dissenters is in the interest of human justice. A moral injustice is committed when people are banned for claims they make, for that would undermine their freedom of expression. Thus, it can be conceived that critique leaves one unsettled and in a state of wandering. It is quite possible to assign new meanings to views espoused – meanings that were not present previously (Rancière, 2011). Here, we specifically think of commenting on students' work and pointing out other meanings that could be linked to the work presented but that students have not given consideration to. Students wander when they think through meanings suggested by supervisors and even come up with their own adjustments to previous arguments.

Thirdly, in my work, I argue for a critique of the self by autonomously bearing witness to one's own writing (Waghid & Davids, 2020). When students testify to their own writing, they question their own writing from the inside instead of relying only on supervisors from outside to point out possible anomalies in their writing. Witnessing allows students to look at their writing in an honest and self-critical way towards writing 'which is still possible and perhaps yet to come' (Waghid & Davids, 2020, p. 54). The point is that critique through witnessing offers one the intellectual and moral space to make decisions on one's work that might be in the interest of the public good. Thus, bearing witness to one's own writing is based on the understanding that one would critically (re)examine one's work in light of new information and claims about knowledge. Next, I show how critique manifested concerning some students' work.

Todd, Benny, and Celia and the art of critique

Todd painstakingly showed how education policy in his home country, Namibia, is intertwined with cultivating democratic citizenship education. He conceptually clarified democratic citizenship education as he endeavoured to proffer his argument that education policy is intertwined with such a notion through analysis and interpretation. What is of interest is that Todd was prepared to look critically at his own work and made adjustments based on more nuanced interpretations of the concept of democratic citizenship education, which he held is misrepresented in education policy initiatives in his country. Consequently, the misconstrued notions of democratic citizenship education have been presented in education policy texts, so teaching and learning at universities have been impacted inappropriately to the extent that teaching and learning as a means to control people seem to remain a dominant educational practice. Todd's self-criticism spurred him on to critically evaluate education policy texts in Namibia and how they adversely impact schooling. In fact, through critique, Todd could ascertain what the conceptual gaps were in education policy texts and then endeavoured how these gaps could be bridged.

Like Todd, Benny also showed how democratic citizenship education, if adjusted to an indigenous perspective in his home country, Ghana, could enhance a more defensible form of societal and moral living. He went on to clarify conceptually how democratic citizenship education impacts a transformative understanding of teaching-learning in secondary schools. He specifically argued why democratic citizenship education offers schools a way to rethink pedagogical action in primary schools. What interests me is the deconstructive way he used a notion of critique to look beyond critical action towards post-critical action in cultivating a more defensible form of schooling in Ghanaian society. The point I am making is that Benny extended his critique based on critiques to find out why transformative teaching-learning can be considered a form of socio-moral action commensurate with a post-critical notion of democratic citizenship education.

Celia produced a doctoral thesis in which she witnessed how critical pedagogy can bring about disruptive action in university education. Not only is her work conceptually rigorous, but it also enables cultivating change in decolonised higher educational contexts. What seems to be quite novel about her work is the way she looked at how decolonisation and critique could co-exist and together bring about disruptive practices in higher education discourses. She used disruption as a conceptual and pragmatic approach to subvert hegemonic forms of higher education. She concluded that resisting dominant higher education discourses is an act of decoloniality whereby people look at emancipatory ways of reconceptualising higher education in Southern Africa.

Summary

I have shown how critique provokes supervisors and students to honour one another's writing and comments on writing respectively. It is unwise to dismiss students' work as irrelevant. Moreover, through wandering, new meanings could be assigned to doctoral work based on putting to question that which is presented. Students invariably make adjustments to their theses based on critical feedback from supervisors. Finally, critique as self-critical thinking allows students to scrutinise their work and make alterations where possible without overwhelmingly relying on supervisors to inform them of doing so – that is, they bear witness to their doctoral work. Students, in turn, are encouraged to witness their own articulations and amend them where possible. In this regard, doctoral writing cannot be separated from a notion of critique.

References

Biesta, G. (2009). Deconstruction, justice, and the vocation of education. In M. A. Peters & G. Biesta (Eds.), *Derrida, deconstruction, and the politics of pedagogy* (pp. 15–38). Peter Lang.

Foucault, M. (1988). *Politics, philosophy, culture: Interviews and other writings 1977–1984* (L. D. Kritzman, Ed.). Routledge.

Masek, A., & Alias, M. (2020). A review of effective doctoral supervision: What is it and how can we achieve it? *Universal Journal of Educational Research, 8*(6), 2493–2500. https://doi.org/10.13189/ujer.2020.080633.

Rancière, J. (2011). The thinking of dissensus: Politics and aesthetics. In P. Bowman & R. Stamp (Eds.), *Reading Rancière: Critical dissensus* (pp. 1–17). Continuum.

Waghid, Y., & Davids, N. (2020). *The thinking university expanded: On profanation, play and education.* Routledge.

9 Doctoral education as profanation and play

Introduction

Doctoral supervision cannot be confined to relations between supervisors and students; the former only ensures that technical procedures and compliance have been followed in writing a doctoral thesis, especially if less emphasis is placed on the arguments that constitute theses. Equally so, I am familiar with several theses where students seem to invest so much time in literature reviews, yet they do not foreground the arguments of scholars in their reviews as if literature analyses are merely pedantic exercises to record what others have said on specific subject matters. If literature reviews are merely written down as conjectures and theoretical postulations of others without connecting one's work with what others have said, then one's own doctoral work would remain truncated and disconnected from the literature. Doctoral theses should show a sense of coherence, implying that an interconnectedness between chapters is necessary. Likewise, arguments have to be foregrounded related to existing theoretical ideas. If not, doctoral work would remain disconnected from significant works that exist. In some way, students must show how their ideas consolidate and/or extend existing arguments in the literature. In this way, literature reviews should not be considered frivolous analyses that have no bearing on current studies. One way of counteracting such ill-advised practices is to disrupt doctoral writing through notions of profanation and play, which will be the discussion that ensues.

Profanation, play, and the disruption of established traditions of writing

Throughout this book, my argument has always been to find a different use for the notion of doctoral supervision. Doctoral supervision cannot be only about effectiveness, as stated here:

> To ensure students graduate on time, institutions are undertaking various measures such as recruiting highly capable candidates, implementing

48 *Doctoral education as profanation and play*

effective thesis supervision and establishing efficient management of doctoral programmes. Among the three measures, the second, i.e. effective supervision has been identified as the key to achieve on-time graduation of candidates enrolled in a doctoral programme.

(Masek & Alias, 2020, p. 2494)

It seems indisputable that doctoral education should be delinked from graduation on time, together with recruiting capable students. However, these are not the only measures that should be attended to in such a form of education. Of course, when students have been recruited, they should be managed so they do not become discouraged about their studies. So what else should be done during doctoral supervision? Accordingly, firstly, I have always been concerned with profanation whereby doctoral supervision will be put to a new use, that is, to liberate things and to return things to a more plausible use (Waghid & Davids, 2020). I specifically think of using the literature review in the doctoral study as an opportunity to accentuate theoretical (re)positioning. That means pointing out the theoretical premises of texts to ascertain where and how doctoral work can be enhanced based on existing theoretical (re)constructs in the literature, say, about the philosophy of higher education. For me, this process of theoretical (re)positioning represents a significant feature of doctoral writing whereby premises of arguments in others' writing are used as an existing platform to proffer one's own new arguments – that is, 'to make coming of a new use possible' (Agamben, 2010, p. 92). I always encourage students to read and (re)interpret works relevant to their own studies. In this way, they should be capable of theoretical (re)positioning so necessary in thesis writing.

Secondly, one of the most challenging aspects of doctoral work is to use the appropriate research methodology for a study. Doctoral work in several higher education studies, certainly in South Africa, seems to be prejudiced towards the use of qualitative approaches to research. In many ways, references to using such approaches seem biased towards including empirical work in theses. So educational research seems to be conceived as studies that must include empirical work of statistical analyses and interviews (individual and group) so that the study looks authentic. I often hear some students talk about the number of institutions and participants that will make up their study as if a reference to empirical work has become the sacred norm. Even during group interviews of students wanting to gain access to our programme, the focus seems to be invariably on numbers and statistics. One way to disrupt the sacred and move towards the profane is to play with doctoral work. Play refers to a process of unconstrained pandemonium that needs to unfold whereby students resist traditional research methods. Giorgio Agamben (2010, p. 92) talks about play as a form of rupturing whereby people make the 'coming of a new use possible'. Much like playing with toys and using the toys for unintended purposes, doctoral educational research should be about resisting familiar ways of doing things to produce more provocative spectres of educational analyses. For example, many higher education studies dealing with the decolonisation of knowledge in Africa should resist established understandings of the concept in favour of profaned notions of decolonisation. For instance, there is nothing spurious about rethinking decolonisation in light of a new form of democratisation that could resist hegemonic discourses.

Thirdly, there seems to be something wrong with doctoral work in a new democratic South Africa that does not take seriously the subversion of unethical life in society. I specifically refer to ongoing instances of racism, discrimination, and exclusion in higher education despite removing apartheid education from the statute books. Hence, I propose that doctoral work in higher education should more pertinently begin to play with an ethic of dignity or *ubuntu* (Waghid, 2022) that takes into controversy higher educational discourses that do not do much about integrating decoloniality into their curricula. As remarked by Waghid (2022, p. 15),

[T]he idea of human dignity ought to be reconsidered in light of a commitment to ensure the well-being of the self in relation to other humans. *Ubuntu* does not just become an expression of and for human dignity but a tangible recognition to ensure the well-being of the self in relation to others.

Next, we show how profanation and play have been enacted concerning some students' work.

Macy, Eddie, and Amy on profanation and play

In her doctoral thesis, Macy developed a defensible form of democratic educational theory that could reconsider private general and further education and training in South Africa. What is interesting about her doctoral study is that she found a new possible use for democratic educational theory. She played with a reconfigured notion of democratic citizenship education and argued how it could reconstitute an understanding of education and training differently. Her thesis also proposed the rupturing of a dichotomy between private and public education by developing a new understanding of what education and training should be.

Eddie offered a provocative analysis of democratic citizenship education and how it can impact higher teaching and learning in accounting education in South Africa. Like Jenny, he proposed a new form of accounting education that addresses a lack of social responsibility. The novelty of his thesis lay in profaning a new understanding of accounting education that ruptures the overwhelming emphasis on technical competence. If South African accounting education were to meaningfully guide transformative human action, it has to be reconstituted within a paradigm of democratic citizenship education.

Amy, in turn, argued for a deliberative theory of education leadership to be coupled with an ethic of *ubuntu*, thus playing with a new use for such an ethic of education. Although the idea of coupling deliberative educational theory and practice with an indigenous concept of knowledge might not have been her own, she used it differently from those thinkers who proposed using a reconceptualised notion of education. She found a new use of deliberative educational theory and how it could guide educational leadership in schools in South Africa.

What is interesting about the aforementioned theses is that profanation and play seem to have guided students' doctoral work, especially regarding a new understanding and use of democratic citizenship education. When Macy, Eddie, and Amy profaned a new use for a notion of democratic citizenship education, they began to play more with the concept concerning educational aspects of their doctoral work.

Summary

In this chapter, I have been concerned with doctoral supervision and writing according to notions of profanation, play, and cultivating a renewed ethic of human dignity (*ubuntu*). Unless a philosophy of higher education does not devote more attention to such actions, doctoral work and its supervision will have failed its graduates. The rationale behind producing more profaned and playful doctoral texts is to develop more credible doctoral studies that stretch the work beyond the mere technical compliance of a doctorate.

References

Agamben, G. (2010). *Profanations* (2nd ed., J. Fort, Trans.). Zone Books.
Masek, A., & Alias, M. (2020). A review of effective doctoral supervision: What is it and how can we achieve it? *Universal Journal of Educational Research*, *8*(6), 2493–2500. https://doi.org/10.13189/ujer.2020.080633
Waghid, Y. (2022). *Education, crisis, and philosophy: Ubuntu within higher education*. Routledge.
Waghid, Y., & Davids, N. (2020). *The thinking university expanded: On profanation, play and education*. Routledge.

10 A personal narrative on doctoral adventures

Introduction

My interest in the African philosophy of higher education provokes me to reconsider doctoral education in the philosophy of higher teaching and learning. I have also pursued doctorate in the philosophy of (higher) education; therefore, my take on such a form of education has a philosophical and higher education bias. As I have shown in the previous two chapters, critique, profanation, and play are important practices in pursuing doctoral studies. Consequently, my own reflections on my doctoral journeys or, as John Murungi (2023) will assert, adventures are not devoid of such actions. In this chapter, I offer a narrative account of my own doctoral adventures, especially highlighting the encounters I pursued in association with my supervisors and some of the challenges I faced regarding paternalism. I focus primarily on the journey's learnings and the cultivation of an African philosophy of higher education. Concomitantly, I also show how I have understood what doctoral writing entails.

An auto-ethnographic account of my doctoral encounters

My initiation into a doctoral pathway was both inspirational and depressing. Having been inspired by a desire to pursue doctoral research, I soon wondered about the possibility of enhancing the philosophy of education as a discourse, and concurrently I tackled a major philosophical problem in Muslim education in South Africa. Thus, I began to venture into the realm of democratic education, intending to change something undesirable in Muslim pedagogical action (Waghid, 1995). For me, conceptual problems in understanding Muslim education in South Africa are the primary reason rigidity unfolded in madrassah (Muslim school) practices. In other words, conceptual problems about higher education influence how learners are taught in schools and the roles teachers take on. And unless the reason for such a form of education could be reconceptualised, Muslim education has little chance that its seemingly

DOI: 10.4324/9781032715872-10

unalterable practices would be changed. Having used a philosophical lens of critical inquiry, I proffered that rigidity in Muslim education ought to be ruptured to impact practices and institutions differently. My encounters with three supervisors were inspired by their interests in the philosophy of education and Muslim education respectively. My supervisors' commitment to the doctoral study and unbridled support contributed significantly to completing the work. Yet equally depressing was that my doctoral work would not be considered hospitable in communities where change was required. Some Muslim communities' persistence with the socialisation of education, often at the expense of critical empowerment and emancipation, has left me somewhat discouraged for years to come. In this way, there seemed to have been some disconnect between my thesis and the communities that needed to undergo some degree of alterity. And I could only have known this because of my personal and professional involvement as a teacher in Muslim schools for more than a decade.

Of course, I consider my doctoral work on Muslim education as an act of decoloniality in the sense that a rigid form of Muslim education that seemed to have subverted autonomous and deliberative learning had to be rethought and practised differently. Like apartheid education constrained autonomous and deliberative action, so Muslim education was hampered by understandings that eroded critical thinking and deliberative engagement among teachers and students. By resisting rigidity and having aimed to reconceptualise Muslim education, my decolonial project seemed to have remained on track. However, without being disingenuous to my supervisors, I did not always feel like an autonomous student. I somehow could sense that I was inhibited from speaking freely and had to look up to my supervisors for constant advice. More specifically, I felt as if I had to acquire, sharpen, and master a brand of philosophy of education known as metatheory that would provide me with the technical skills and scientific approach to pursue credible doctoral work.

As an African doctoral student, I somehow experienced a paternal attitude towards my thinking and writing, which invariably compromised my autonomy as a student. It seemed as if my ethical agency as a student was compromised by what appears to have been the enthusiasm of instructive supervisors who deemed it defensible to generate advice they deemed good for my learning and development. Only when I pursued a post-doctoral fellowship at a highly acclaimed Muslim higher educational institution in Malaysia did I recognise how ethically problematic paternalism was during my doctoral studies. Under the tutelage of its founder director, Professor Dr Syed Naquib al-Attas, I learned through attending his lectures that human thought should be left unconstrained so that new breakthroughs in human understanding could be forthcoming. As I am authoring this section, I have just been informed by a friend, Professor Wan Muhammad Nor Wan Daud of al-Attas's new publication at the age of 92. In Islam: the Covenants Fulfilled (Al-Attas, 2023) is considered by the author as an inspirational discourse that invites readers to ethically discern and reason:

> When I was writing this discourse, explaining the results of my investigations to my students and followers of intelligence and discernment, I told them that this discourse was for me as a journey along the lowlands, across the foothills, and over the mountain peaks of thoughts discovering astonishing events that occurred in the past effecting the present without altering the future in that which has already been recognized and acknowledged by the Muslim *ummah* as the truth. I was aware that God prompted me to go on with this journey to the very end, and aided me as the occasion demands with inspired knowledge confirmed by veridical feeling to gather together the separate discoveries till they fit into one another as a comprehensive whole. I have done that. My intelligent and discerning readers will be able to confirm what I just said by the time they reach the end of this discourse.
>
> (Al-Attas, 2023: Preface)

Again in 2000, I embarked on a doctoral journey in which I emphasised the significance of reflexive democratic practices in transforming higher teaching-learning (Waghid, 2001). What seemed to have guided this study was an understanding that unless university education was equally attentive to research, teaching-learning, and community engagement, it would fail to serve the public good. This novel idea has subsequently been used in major works about such an understanding of the university in South Africa. That is, to intertwine teaching-learning, educational research, and community engagement is a realisation that teaching-learning is a research endeavour, whereas educational research is constituted by a notion of teaching-learning. Similarly, community engagement is a teaching-learning action and simultaneously also a research endeavour. In this way, no separation is made between various concepts of university education. My encounter with my supervisor at the time was fairly engaging. In fact, I am persuaded that my understanding of deliberative democracy in the early 2000s impacted how the department where I work began to rethink its notion of social democracy related to university education and schooling. However, the ramifications of the encounter did not extend to the academic challenges and complexities that confronted the faculty at a time when dissent was seemingly considered an impossibility. This is also one of the reasons I decided to embark on this doctoral journey, besides my optimism to publicise my thoughts. Not only would I enhance my research capacities and skills to examine education policy studies, but pursuing a doctorate at the university where I now work would, so it seemed at the time, increase my credibility as a scholar at the institution. No longer could colleagues question my credentials from a different institution, but more importantly, acquiring a qualification in the department where I now worked gave me much more acceptability among my colleagues. And considering that my supervisor was my departmental head and immediately rebuffed any criticism that I was inadequately initiated to teach in the faculty. The parochial view that an academic who did not acquire a qualification from the institution where I work could not be a good university teacher was once and for all dispelled, at least, so it seemed at the time. I am not suggesting that achieving some qualification at the institution where one works should be a prerequisite for good teaching. On the contrary, a further examination into a discourse of teaching-learning that aims to democratise university practices can contribute to cultivating democratic action. But to acquire a formal qualification might not be necessary to enhance such knowledge claims.

After being told that the department where I worked required more philosophical analyses in their academic work, I was motivated to embark on another doctoral journey. This time, journey was in political philosophy in the department of philosophy at the university I worked. Having been supervised by a demanding and rigorous scholar, my doctorate was actualised with a focus on the importance of communitarian thought in human educational discourses. It was then that my understanding of democratic action took a post-structuralist turn: democratic action can no longer just be attentive to the critical liberation of social institutions and practices; it also needed to be considered deconstructively for breakthroughs and openings to manifest in iterative discourses. My understanding of autonomy, community, and transformation became prejudiced towards cultivating justice, equality, and unconstrained freedom in society (Waghid, 2002). However, besides my interest in political philosophy, the assumption that Africans require catching up with those who are developed inspired me the most to pursue a doctorate in political philosophy – of course, I would not say that I required catching up. Murungi (2023, p. 103) explains ethically flawed paternalism as follows:

> Africans, as is the case of most people in the developing world are, then, expected to imitate or catch up with those who are developed. The good they are socialized to pursue is the good that is synonymous with the good as conceived in the so-called development world.

At the time, it did seem quite demeaning to assert that the philosophy of education, as practised in the department where I work, was not on par with philosophy in the university's philosophy department. Of course, doing philosophy of education is not the same as practising philosophy. When one practises the philosophy of education, one analyses concepts and practices pertaining to educational aspects of societal life. Doing philosophy does not specifically involve analyses of education but also other fields of inquiry such as ethics, business, and politics. Philosophy of education involves analyses of problems and to examine their implications for education. However, to claim that one requires philosophy from a specific department amounts to the domestication of philosophy itself. It is tantamount to arguing that one would not be doing genuine philosophy of education if it is not practised in exactly the same way a specific department does. And, as it might have been the case, the department where I eventually studied mostly practised philosophy grounded in Euro-Western thought. Considering that a Euro-Western approach to philosophy is different from a decolonised approach to philosophy, one can argue that such a form of philosophy could have biased the 'Europeanisation of Africa' (Murungi, 2023, p. 97), which in itself is a form of neo-colonisation. My understanding of philosophy is that it ought to respond to claims of exclusion, marginalisation, and domination. If philosophy cannot be responsive to such societal repressive matters, there seems to be no point in practising a decolonised notion of philosophy.

The aforementioned doctoral journeys provide some philosophical, educational, and moral premises, according to which I currently analyse societal dystopias on the African continent and consider their implications for higher education. Thus, nowadays, when I speak about an African philosophy of higher education, I refer to an analysis of major problems on the continent and a (re)consideration of its implications for university education. It is such a notion of African philosophy of higher education that seems to be commensurate with the enactment of reasonable, caring, compassionate, just, and equal human action attuned to a notion of *ubuntu* (autonomous, dignified, and interdependent human action) (Waghid, 2014). By implication, in a reconsidered view of the African philosophy of higher education, I argue that reasoned, caring, dignified, compassionate, equal, free, and just human actions ought to be intertwined with an ethic of *ubuntu* that can enhance thinking with-in and about higher pedagogy.

Subsequently, my scholarly work in the field of African philosophy of higher education over almost three decades has emerged as a communitarian and moral response to social dystopias on the African continent. More recently, I combined three ethical practices, namely *ubuntu* (human dignity and interdependence), *ukama* (relationality), and *umsebenzi* (activism), in relation to higher teaching-learning to show how an African philosophy of higher education manifests (Waghid, 2023). Yet my advocacy for an *ubuntu* university embraces actions such as autonomy, iteration, and responsibility in the quest to harness what a university on the African continent should stand for (Waghid et al., 2023). The idea of an African philosophy of higher education is constituted by three constitutive meanings: *ubuntu* (human dignity and interdependence), *ukama* (relationality), and *umsebenzi* (activism). Through *ubuntu*, humans act with the decorum of integrity and honour towards themselves and other humans; *ukama* connects them through iterations based on claims of reasonableness and cultural expressions; and *umsebenzi* provokes them (humans) to act decently in the pursuit of actively responding to and subverting forms of oppression, colonialism, and racism pertaining to higher educational discourses.

Cultivating decoloniality through (post)doctoral education

Earlier, I have alluded to the fact that the philosophy (of higher education) in Southern Africa seems skewed towards Euro-Westernism and the Europeanisation of Africa. What is wrong with teaching a philosophy (of higher education) aimed at cultivating Euro-Western paternalism? Having a cursory look at the German philosopher Georg Hegel's (1770–1831) depiction of Africans, it appears he believed that they were not human and exhibited recklessness and barbarity. His degradation of Africans as non-human savages and heathens is a vindication of the disregard he had shown towards an African philosophy (of higher education) (Hegel, 1888, p. 21). The upshot of this argument is that, if an African philosophy of higher education were to succeed, it has to become predominantly Euro-Western. Many higher education institutions in Southern Africa seem influenced by Hegelian thought that depicts African philosophy (of higher education) as truncated and underdeveloped. And, as implied by Murungi (2023), such an understanding of African philosophy (of higher education) seems too dependent on Euro-Western philosophy (of higher education).

For instance, for many years, my own standing as an African philosopher of higher education was conceived by some Euro-Western scholars as underdeveloped; hence, I would hear remarks about my Google citations that were surprisingly minimal compared to those of established scholars, whoever they might be. Similarly, I was once questioned by a European philosopher of education whether all Muslims hold the view that education should be subjected to deliberative engagement as if a philosophy of Muslim education cannot be conceived of as encouraging iteration among humans. Even at my first international philosophy of education conference held in Johannesburg in 1996, a Euro-Western scholar reminded me that my views on openness and reflexivity in (Muslim) education would lead to my incarceration in a Muslim-dominated country on the African continent. Thus, it seemed as if my post-doctoral understanding of the philosophy of higher education in Africa was considered either too underdeveloped by some or too radical by others. In addition, my own analysis of a Kantian notion of critique also questioned some of the discriminatory murmurs about his sense of reason. That Kant considered Africans as intellectually underdeveloped (Kant, 2004) is a view that undermines Kantian ethics and brings this illustrious scholar's reputation into disrepute. If Kant's derogatory claims about Africans have been made so pronounced, then the possibility exists that Kantian philosophers would discount any notion of African philosophy (of higher education). In other words, it is not uncommon for some Western European scholars to discredit anything African, specifically an African philosophy of higher education. As stated by Ejeh (2022, p. 10),

> Our study reveals that Kant's ethical theory or the categorical imperative does not apply to Africa and other non-white races because Kant

denies Africans, women, and other non-whites the ability to reason or rationalise, which according to Kant, is the criterion for being moral. In other words, the work reveals that Kant does not consider Africans as moral agents, and since they are not moral agents, they are simply brutes.

Thus, it does appear as if my understanding of an African philosophy of higher education has become vulnerable to some dehumanising understanding of higher education. That is, understanding that my views on decolonising higher education so that all humans could freely express themselves seemed to have been suppressed by some because of its alignment with critical discourses of higher education. I always believed that (post)doctoral education cannot ignore the pursuit of what is genuinely good for human well-being. And that meant that a philosophy of higher education in Africa should truly encourage peace and vehemently oppose unjust wars, dictatorial regimes, the brutalisation of innocent people, and the deprivation of freedom on the African continent (Waghid, 2023). Only then would the decoloniality of higher education become realisable.

Furthermore, the crisis of coloniality in Southern Africa persists. As Aime Cesaire (2001) so aptly reminds us, Africans continue to experience the burdens of enslavement and dehumanisation as a consequence of violating their human rights. I remember the resistance of some scholars towards the notion of an African philosophy of (higher) education based on a spurious assumption that such a philosophy is prone to irrationality and superstition. Not only is such a criticism invalid, but it is actually directed at a notion of ethnophilosophy that embraces people's cultures, languages, and ethnicities. Now to assume that philosophy can be distanced from people's contexts is to be oblivious that humans are constituted in contexts, and what makes them what they are is ontologically linked to where they come from. In my academic relationships with some international scholars, I always felt intuitively as if they considered Africans as people who required additional support, similar to the view advocated by Kant that Africans are not human. Consequently, my students and I considered our doctoral educational encounters as pedagogical adventures of reciprocity constituted by mutual respect and the recognition of one another as legitimate participants in such encounters. Therefore, the point of accentuating an African philosophy of higher education is threefold. Firstly, it is an affirmation that such a philosophy of higher education exists in Africa, and rightly so. Any attempt to disparage such a philosophy of higher education can only be assumed to be discriminatory and racist; secondly, such a philosophy of higher education is meant to decolonise dominant discourses on (higher) education; thirdly, an African philosophy of higher education seems to be the continent's most appropriate philosophy to respond to crises of dictatorships, dehumanisation, and torture.

Summary

My own doctoral narrative corroborates my interests in the African philosophy of higher education, interspersed with arguments in and about the cultivation of democratic citizenship and cosmopolitan education. Much of my doctoral work extended into a higher teaching-learning discourse in which notions of quality, equality, equity, freedom, democracy, citizenship, cosmopolitanism, and justice seem to have actualised in their potentiality. In the main, these concepts remain in potentiality as I endeavour to make more philosophical advances in our scholarly work. My reflexive analyses intimate that the African philosophy of higher education remains in becoming. And any attempt to rethink an African philosophy of higher education cannot be separated from the socio-political and moral premises of what higher education means.

References

Al-Attas, S. M. N. (2023). *Islam: The covenants fulfilled.* Ta'dib Publishing.
Cesaire, A. (2001). *Discourse on colonialism* (J. Pinkham, Trans.). Monthly Review Foundation.
Ejeh, C. P. (2022). Kant's racial views and the categorical imperative. *Philosophy International Journal, 5*(2), 1–10.
Hegel, G. (1888). *Introduction to the philosophy of history* (J. Sibree, Trans.). Bell and Daldy.
Kant, I. (2004). *Observations on the feeling of the beautiful and sublime* (J. T. Goldthwait, Trans.). University of California Press.
Murungi, J. (2023). *African philosophical adventures.* Lexington Books.
Waghid, Y. (1995). *Are problems in South African Madaris due to an inadequate concept of Madrassah schooling?* (Unpublished doctoral thesis). University of the Western Cape.
Waghid, Y. (2001). *A conceptual analysis of a reflexive democratic praxis related to higher education transformation in South Africa* (Unpublished doctoral thesis). Stellenbosch University.
Waghid, Y. (2002). *Community and democracy in South Africa: Liberal versus communitarian perspectives* (Unpublished doctoral thesis). Stellenbosch University.
Waghid, Y. (2014). *African philosophy of education reconsidered: On being human.* Routledge.
Waghid, Y. (2023). *Chronicles on African philosophy of higher education: A colloquy among friends.* Brill.
Waghid, Y., Hungwe, J., Shawa, L. B., Terblanche, J., Waghid, Z., & Waghid, F. (2023). *Towards an ubuntu university: African higher education reimagined.* Palgrave Macmillan.

11 On questioning reasoned and democratic universities

Towards an *ubuntu* university

Introduction

My exposition of doctoral supervision cannot be confined to discussing the relations between supervisors and students. One would be remiss of the context where such supervision unfolds. As I endeavoured to make sense of my supervisory actions, I invariably had at the back of my mind an understanding of a university in which supervision could be enacted and flourished. Therefore, in this chapter, I exposit how my understanding of a university has shifted over the last three decades, specifically invoking three types of universities that informed my thinking: a reasoned university, a democratic university, and an *ubuntu* university. It is to such an analysis that I now turn my attention.

Revisiting a reasoned university

A university is what it is based on the reasons that constitute it. To talk about a university is to invoke notions of discernment and judgement. Discernment and judgement constitute what a university is, or more specifically, it provides a university with capacities to enact reason. A discerning university makes up its erudite and intellectual status, whereas a judging university involves the knowledgeability and intelligence of the higher education institution. In this way, a reasoned university is constituted by discernment and judgement – erudition and knowledgeability. In both instances, discernment and judgement, as well as erudition and knowledgeability, the actions of humans are invoked. That is, humans (university teachers and students) are reasonable beings that give universities their discerning (erudite) and judging (knowledgeable) actions. Put differently, a reasoned university is what it is on account of teachers' and students' exercise of discerning and judging capacities as they pursue intellectualism and knowledgeableness. In turn, a university of discernment and judgement remains open to critique – that is, argumentation and dissonance (Derrida, 2004). So, when academics exercise their reason, they judge, criticise, and take risks in the corroboration of their arguments. They autonomously exercise their reason and freely enact their moral judgements (Waghid & Davids, 2020). In this regard, Jacques Derrida makes the following claim about a reasoned university:

> [The reasoned university] is there, to tell the truth, to judge, to criticise in the most rigorous sense of the term, namely to discern and decide between the true and the false; and if it is also entitled to decide between the just and the unjust, the moral and the immoral, this is insofar as reason and freedom of judgement are implicated as well.
>
> (Derrida, 2004, p. 97)

With a university's concern with reasoned action, it (a university) also positions itself in relation to its public responsibility (Simons et al., 2007). In this way, a reasoned university does not only discern and judge but also responds in relation to what is good for the public or society. Considering societies worldwide are in perpetual transition due to technological innovations and societal dystopias, it seems apposite for reasoned universities to respond to such innovations and dystopias. Recently, there has been much debate about using the AI ChatGPT programme in universities and the possibility that academic plagiarism might escalate, together with deliberations about ongoing ethnic conflict and war in some parts of Africa. Universities of reason are now challenged to respond to such innovations and dystopias respectively.

The point about a reasoned university is that judgements are proffered in defence of what such a university and its academics and students do. No action ensues in the public without a university providing reasons for such action to occur. Of course, not all societal actions necessarily depend on what reasoned universities come up with. However, when societies act upon university education, reasons will be provided to ensure its implementation is credible. On the contrary, our potential critic might legitimately pose the question: How is it possible for reasoned universities to flourish in (Southern) Africa when, as posited by Philip Altbach (2007, p. 222), '[m]ost African governments are intolerant of dissent, criticism, non-conformity, and free expression of controversial, new, or unconventional ideas'? I agree that serious violations of freedom of expression do exist, and the possibility that academics be silenced by security forces and militant groups is real and oppositional to reason. And I acknowledge that dissenting academics who speak out often are tortured, terrorised, incarcerated, and expelled (Altbach, 2007). Yet reasoned universities continue to exist in the face of societal upheavals, political instabilities, economic uncertainties, persecutions, and adverse working and living conditions (Altbach, 2007). In other words, societal dystopias erode the use of reason at African universities – that is, reason is still present but at a minimal level.

Towards a democratic university

Over the last two decades, in particular, universities have emerged as institutions prepared to combine their concern with economic prosperity and societal welfare development coupled with the cultivation of education for democratic citizenship. In the words of Maartin Simons (Simons et al., 2007, p. 442), knowledge societies need

> [a]n optimal mobilization of useful brainpower in order to bring about economic prosperity (through research-based innovation, sustainable employability), social welfare (through knowledge-based regional development, increased higher education attainment), and democratic participation (through the promotion of citizenship competencies).

Bearing in mind the above, some universities have evolved as democratic higher education institutions, intent on serving the economy and society in which they are situated. The democratic university relies on iterative action among its academics and students to advance its performativity or what Jean-Francois Lyotard (1984) refers to as the commercialisation of knowledge for its entrepreneurial ends. Every academic activity in a democratic university seems linked to measurable outcomes, whether research outputs, student throughputs, and academic and support staffing. For instance, a faculty's viability as a functioning unit in the university is negotiated based on its knowledge interests vis-à-vis its economic sustainability. The number of academic courses, programmes, and/or modules a faculty offers depends on the centralised funding received from the university's management and, of course, negotiated with deans who often become the middle managers to ensure that the corporatist agenda of the university is advanced. In many ways, a democratic university (certainly in Southern Africa) has succumbed to the neoliberal ideals of efficiency and effectiveness based on the availability of funds and the presence of democratic arrangements to justify funding allocations, for instance, to faculty. Nowadays, a democratic university appoints a few popular academics who can increase the institution's visibility and marketability (with little consultation, I must add) at exorbitant costs to the institution. Gone are the production of knowledge for its own sake and the reluctance to take up controversial matters of interest to the wider public. My point is that critique and subversiveness are no longer associated with the scholarship of uncritical academics who refuse to take up a position (Derrida, 2004). Under the guise of democratic iterations, some academics have become complacent and unresponsive to real societal issues because it is too much of a (financial) risk to assume controversial positions. As aptly remarked by Giroux and Searls-Giroux (2004, p. 278):

> Making no connections to audiences outside of the academy or to the issues that bear down on their everyday lives, these academics have

become largely irrelevant. This is not to suggest that they do not publish or speak at symposiums but that they often do so to limited audiences and in a language that is overly abstract, highly aestheticized, rarely takes an overtly political position, and seems largely indifferent to broader public issues.

It is not that a democratic university is flawed, but rather, its performative-managerialist agenda seems to have catapulted the higher educational institution's extrinsic purposes. Under the aegis of democratic ideals, many Southern African universities have succumbed to the demands of a global market economy, emphasising the commodification of knowledge, privatisation of higher education, institutional and individual rankings, and educational outcomes. In many ways, some democratic universities are remiss of their public and moral responsibilities as higher education institutions. Often many popular academics speak out on issues that do not seem to be controversial. But when it comes to matters that require their moral integrity to respond, a deafening silence will befall us.

For example, a lot is said about marginalising the indigenous Afrikaans language at the institution I am affiliated with. However, there seems to be no comment about violent conflict in some African countries. Not that the seeming marginalisation of the Afrikaans language is unimportant. However, when an institution becomes selective about voicing its dissent without responding to broader issues on the continent, such a university seems to turn a blind eye to significant developments. Next, I talk about the notion of an *ubuntu* university.

Cultivating an *ubuntu* university

Elsewhere I make a comprehensive argument for the notion of an *ubuntu* university (Waghid et al., 2023). I argue that a university like this embodies objective reason, conscience, and humility (Waghid et al., 2023). A university that encourages objective reasoning is one where people act autonomously in association with one another. That is, teachers and students are free to speak in collaboration with one another. Acting with a conscience is a substantive ethical commitment towards the university and its surroundings so that teachers and students have a moral responsibility towards the institution and society. And a university of humility is attentive to human indignity and suffering (Waghid et al., 2023). In these ways, a university of *ubuntu* is concerned with people's autonomy and collaboration, institutional and public responsibility, and resistance to human injustice and humiliation. The point is that an *ubuntu* university uses its capacity to reason to enhance autonomous and deliberative action, public responsibility, and an opposition to human indignity, suffering, and torture.

Secondly, an *ubuntu* university is concerned with cultivating indaba – that is, deliberation, freedom of expression, communalism, and equality (Waghid et al., 2023). In this way, the democratic orientation of an *ubuntu* university is quite evident. *Indaba* is a Zulu/Nguni term that accentuates openness, deliberative iteration, and unconstrained speech articulation in engaged actions (Waghid et al., 2023). Consequently, an *ubuntu* university of *indaba* recognises the importance of democratic procedures in the enactment of higher education matters. What is quite interesting about an *ubuntu* university is that it combines indigenous practices with democratic actions, that is, indaba with a notion of iterative action to make the case of an *ubuntu* university.

Thirdly, cultivating caring and humanity is considered a substantive function of an *ubuntu* university (Waghid et al., 2023). Unlike the reasoned and democratic universities concerned mostly with advancing managerial and performative concerns, the caring and humane university not only opposes such neoliberal ideals but also works earnestly in enacting the institution's and society's decolonisation. More specifically, decolonisation seems to be concerned with resisting the hegemony of one over another. Talking about the decolonisation of university education denotes a resistance to disrupt misconstrued practices that constitute university education. Along with decolonisation, decoloniality is used to restore marginalised communities' cultural values, economic aspirations, and knowledge interests. As stated elsewhere:

> By implication, the decolonisation of the public university is an attempt to oppose and undermine the imperialist legacy and devaluation of the cultures and knowledge interests of marginalised communities. Decolonisation of higher education thus involves recognising the cultural values and knowledge concerns of marginalised communities that have been suppressed and undermined. In this way, the decolonisation of higher education can be couched as a rearticulation of the underlying value systems of excluded communities. And, this is where the decolonisation project connects with *ubuntu* in the sense that the latter equally insists that the values of the other in their otherness should be attended to. Hence, the decolonisation of higher education is synonymous with reshaping the higher education landscape according to the moral values of *ubuntu*.
> (Waghid et al., 2023, p. 125)

Southern African universities seemed to have found a reason in *ubuntu* to reorganise their practices in line with decolonised actions. Although an African university still seeks recognition for its reasoned activities, it does not in its entirety want to surrender to neoliberal ideals. And, for this to happen, it seems to have found some connection with *ubuntu*. Yet we still have a while before notions of an *ubuntu* university really manifest in Southern African higher education institutions. Critics of an *ubuntu* university are adamant that such a university will privilege non-reasoned and non-democratic thinking.

On the contrary, through the notion of *ubuntu*, reason is accentuated, iterative action encouraged, and responsiveness to what is still to come is enhanced.

Summary

In this chapter, I questioned the notions of reasoned and democratic universities in Southern Africa that seem to prejudice such higher education institutions' performative and managerial aspirations. These understandings of a university undermine the credentials of authentic universities on the African continent and mitigate the aspirations of genuine transformative universities oppositional to the further colonisation and subjugation of the knowledge interests of such higher education institutions. Hence, I have proffered a defence of an *ubuntu* university that uses its reasoned and democratic pedigrees to cultivate a university of conscience, dignity, *indaba*, caring, and humaneness in response to societal dystopias confronting African societies.

In my view, the notion of an *ubuntu* university provides the context in which doctoral supervision along the lines of autonomous, iterative, and restorative action can most appropriately be exercised. The latter claim shall be examined in the next chapter.

References

Altbach, P. G. (2007). *Tradition and transition: The international imperative in higher education*. Sense Publishers.
Derrida, J. (2004). *Eyes of the university: Right to philosophy 2* (J. Plug et al., Trans.). Stanford University Press.
Giroux, H. A., & Searls-Giroux, S. (2004). *Take back higher education: Race, youth, and the crisis of democracy in the post-civil rights era*. Palgrave Macmillan.
Lyotard, J. F. (1984). *Postmodern condition: A report on knowledge*. University of Minnesota Press.
Simons, M., Haverhals, B., & Biesta, G. (2007). Introduction: The university revisited. *Studies in Philosophy and Education, 26*, 395–404.
Waghid, Y., & Davids, N. (2020). *The thinking university expanded*. Routledge.
Waghid, Y., Terblanche, J., Shawa, L., Hungwe, T., Waghid, F., & Waghid, Z. (2023). *Towards an ubuntu university: African higher education reimagined*. Palgrave Macmillan.

12 On autonomous, iterative, and restorative doctoral supervision

A glimpse into the future

Introduction

Based on years of experience supervising doctoral students, I offer some conceptual-pragmatic framework of how doctoral supervision can be actualised in its potentiality. I am attracted to the notion of an *ubuntu* university that also provides three analysis points for which doctoral supervision should unfold: autonomous, iterative, and restorative action. If I encountered one more doctoral student and she had to be the last one I had to supervise, I would follow a procedure grounded in what it means to enact autonomous, iterative, and restorative action.

Doctoral supervision in becoming: on autonomous, iterative, and restorative action

Considering that many of my students come from Southern Africa, I expect them to have at least some understanding of what constitutes an African philosophy of higher education. If they are unfamiliar with any notion of an African philosophy of higher education, I would refer them to my edited book, *Chronicles on African Philosophy of Higher Education: A Colloquy Among Friends* (Waghid, 2023), in which I argue for an African philosophy of higher education constituted by notions of democratic iterations, co-belonging, and critique within human encounters. I contend that these moral and intellectual touchstones of an African philosophy of higher education can perpetuate a notion of reflexive activism whereby people can act freely, communally, caringly, and liberatory within and beyond their higher educational encounters. Reflexive activism provokes people to act autonomously and communally, learning to live with differences and otherness, and enacting caring rhythmically among themselves (Waghid, 2023). Bearing in mind that reflexive activism is a form of epistemological, ethical, and political resistance that undermines societal dystopias, an African philosophy of higher education becomes a defensible rationale for which doctoral pursuits in Africa should be undertaken.

DOI: 10.4324/9781032715872-12

What does one do to engage students autonomously, iteratively, and restoratively? Firstly, the student (Hannah) and I would meet at a local coffee shop where we would present ourselves to one another. During our first meeting, we would familiarise ourselves with one another's knowledge interests. As a supervisor, I would listen attentively to what Hannah has to say without passing judgement on every word she articulates. When students speak freely, they develop the confidence to speak without interruption and have to be unduly concerned about how they speak. Their openness and willingness to speak and share their thoughts on a potential doctoral investigation are undoubtedly their initiation into doctoral studies. Without steering and dominating the encounter, I subtly ask them questions about the books they read and what excites them the most about reading specific books. I would speak frankly and cordially when a moment in our encounter arises where Hannah asks my opinion about her understanding of an educational matter she would want to pursue in her studies. I aim not to put Hannah off or discourage her from pursuing her doctoral dream. Rather, I want her to be driven innately so that doctoral studies would become a matter of intrinsic satisfaction in addition to the extrinsic reward such a qualification would offer. In this way, Hannah's subjectivity would become the main driving force as to why a doctoral qualification should be pursued. How she subjectively understands higher education in Africa and what she hopes to accomplish with her investigation become the primary focus of our educational encounter. After an hour of talking and drinking tea and coffee with a muffin and scone, Hannah decided that her meeting with me had taken enough of our time, and we jointly agreed that she would send us tentative thoughts in writing what she envisages to do in her study.

Towards a doctoral proposal . . .

After at least two weeks since my first encounter, I would remind Hannah to send me her thoughts in writing, not necessarily in the formal proposal format. On receiving Hannah's tentative thoughts, I would look out for at least three possible things: the possibility that a question can be asked about an educational matter – that is, the epistemological question; that a mode of inquiry is present in her writing – that is the theoretical-cum-conceptual paradigm for the inquiry, and that her references are credible – that is, some of the technical requirements for thesis writing are adhered to. As a philosophy of higher education student, Hannah is expected to share her provisional thoughts on a real-life situation in a university classroom or the wider society. I want Hannah to share a real-life situation she envisages philosophising – that is, to make real claims about a particular educational matter and proffer some tentative arguments to defend her claims. Only after she has shared a real philosophical problem about an institution or society with me would I encourage her to think about ideas in the sky, as informed by philosophical readings in and about a particular educational matter. For instance, for Hannah to escape the murkiness of reality to the ideal implies that Hannah has to find a way to reconcile ideas in the sky with those on Earth. Jacques Rancière (2010) refers to such a way of doing as reconciling two opposite theses: to escape the greyness of reality on Earth into the ideal and to return from the ideal sky back to reality.

I am specifically thinking of theses addressing a political conundrum in several African countries related to a lack of participation in democratic citizenry. The expectation is that students would identify the dominance of authoritarianism in society and then examine its implications for higher education – a matter of doing African philosophy of higher education. I am interested to know how students formulate their research questions and how they would respond to the problem(s) they have identified. Put differently, I am interested in students' methodological positioning. Because the cultivation of democratic citizenship education relates to human empowerment and emancipation in society, I encourage my students to use a critical education theoretical framework to ascertain how the problem of authoritarianism can be mitigated. In this way, most of my students use a critical and post-critical methodological paradigm to rethink major philosophical problems and then examine their implications for higher education. In this way, students would have conjured up three important aspects of their research proposal: (1) the research question, (2) methodology, and (3) consideration of the implications of the study for higher education.

Once Hannah has communicated her three key areas of investigation, based on my feedback, I encourage her to produce a fully-fledged research proposal for doctoral studies. This would imply that the research questions, coupled with their methodological requirements and consideration of their ramifications for higher education, would now be augmented according to (4) the motivation and rationale of the study, (5) some tentative theoretical remarks on the study (often known as a preliminary literature review), (6) scope and extensiveness of the study, and (7) some timeline for the investigation. All in all, a doctoral research proposal including references should not exceed 6,000 to 8,000 words – that is, usually the word limit for some academic journals.

From proposal submission to iterative action . . .

After I read and commented on Hannah's revised proposal, I arranged an oral examination for her to defend her proposal. This defence is an attempt to go beyond the autonomous creative will of a student towards subjecting her work to the critical scrutiny of others – a matter of moving into the realm of iterative action. Whereas the doctoral proposal is an embodiment of the student who puts her stamp on the study, the oral defence of the proposal is a moment through which the student's ownership of the proposal is subjected to probing by others. It begins an iterative process of reading, critiquing, and commenting on Hannah's work. Of course, the authorial rights of Hannah never vanish, but she becomes less and less attached to considering her thesis as the dominant text that cannot be shattered by her readers, particularly me, the supervisor.

The practice of iteration is meant to liberate a doctoral study from 'the aura of a unique work' (Rancière, 2010, p. 102). Put differently, a doctorate is an argumentative study that cannot be associated with originality connected with the myth of an author-student who produces exemplary and flawless work. Unimpeachable work does not exist to make sense of it, as no text can be beyond suspicion and criticism. It is through iterative action that Hannah and I can engage one another about her writing and proffering of arguments. Yet the proffering of arguments should cohere, and therefore, it seems plausible to (8) organise a doctorate in themes or chapters that are methodically consistent. Iterative action implies that the doctoral text and integrated themes/chapters are invariably subjected to critical scrutiny by myself and/or external readers. Only after a (9) first draft of the doctoral thesis is produced can the question be asked about its (10) restorative possibility. Practically all the theses I supervised related to restoring an impoverished situation in higher teaching-learning. More recently, my students' philosophical contributions involved reconceptualising teaching-learning in university education. I have seen theses that advance a notion of teaching-learning as provocation-evocation (Waghid et al., 2018). What I would be interested in is how Hannah, as my future student, would advance higher teaching-learning beyond provocation-evocation.

Being concerned with the restorative possibility of a doctoral thesis is a matter of coming up with a text and arguments whose legitimacy coincides with what it means for institutions and practices to adapt, reconstruct, or transform. Whatever is at stake will hopefully be responded to by the doctoral arguments that will institute a space for what is still to come free of perplexity. For instance, most of the doctoral theses supervised by me involved in cultivating democratic citizenship education in universities and the broader African society. Basically, the doctoral theses of my students should be able to respond restoratively to shattered institutions of higher education and their concomitant practices.

Summary

In the main, autonomous, iterative, and restorative doctoral theses are constituted by ten intellectual and moral touchstones of thesis writing: question(s), methodology, innuendo, raison d'être, theory, realm, timeline, themes, draft(s), and restoration. Without such gems, it is seemingly unlikely that a doctoral thesis would be actualised in its potentiality. My commitment towards doctoral education remains in becoming, and I still have much to offer in this field of educational inquiry. I hope to continue my doctoral pursuits and open up opportunities for further philosophical and moral reflectiveness and (post) critical scrutiny.

References

Rancière, J. (2010). *Chronicles of consensual times*. Continuum.
Waghid, Y. (Ed.). (2023). *Chronicles on African philosophy of higher education: A colloquy among friends*. Brill.
Waghid, Y., Waghid, F., & Waghid, Z. (2018). *Rupturing African philosophy on teaching and learning: Ubuntu justice and education*. Palgrave Macmillan.

13 On decolonised doctoral education

Introduction

It might appear that the Council on Higher Education's (CHE, 2022) report on doctoral education in South Africa is a confirmation that doctoral studies are in a quandary. And the reasons cited for such a dilemma might be actual reasons that attest to the precariousness of the doctoral situation in the country. I do not deny the absence of policies and procedures relevant to doctoral studies; a lack of formal agreements between supervisors and students; clear outcomes of student performance; monitored student progress; adequate student (and supervisor) training in the ethics processes and research integrity required for the doctoral research projects; prepared students in doctoral programmes; and formally established and well-functioning higher degrees committee (or equivalent name) to oversee a doctoral programme (CHE, 2022). Likewise, as noted by Chaya Herman (2017), doctoral education in South Africa seems to be in a quandary because, for many years, it has been stunted by exclusivity, discrimination, and the absence of a doctoral culture exacerbated by inadequate funding, a small pool of students, high attrition rates, and limited supervisory capacity. Similarly, Nico Cloete, Johann Mouton, and George Sheppard (2015) accentuate the dire situation of doctoral education in Africa, particularly related to a shortage of funding; low institutional capacity; lack of diversity and duplication of programmes; poor-quality supervision; inadequate responsiveness to national, social, and economic needs; weak links to industry; and a lack of academic freedom.

All these might be legitimate reasons why the doctorate is in a dilemma in the country. Yet these are not the most important reasons doctoral education is seemingly at a crossroads in the country. My contention is, and as I consistently argued throughout this book, that doctoral education seems remiss of wonder, wander, and whisper. These action concepts provide sufficient justification as to why doctoral programmes in the country need to be reconceptualised. If any doctoral pursuit does not consider wonder, wander, and whisper as legitimate reasons for wanting to embark on a doctoral study, then such qualifications are really in peril.

DOI: 10.4324/9781032715872-13

Why is doctoral education in South Africa really in peril?

When actions such as wonder, wander, and whisper are missing from doctoral studies, the problem with doctoral education is not empirical but a conceptual or philosophical predicament. A philosophical dilemma exists if students and supervisors do not consider wonder, wander, and whisper significant epistemological actions to guide doctoral studies. It is like saying doctorates do not need philosophy. Really? If doctorates are produced without wonder, wander, and whisper, what is the point of such doctorates? It is tantamount to asserting that unthinkable doctorates are possible. However, the absence of philosophical rigour from doctorates is not just some casual admission of error. Instead, it intimates that such doctorates do not venture into playing off risks against one another (Derrida, 2004). If a doctorate has no inkling of putting up one argument against another and ascertaining which argument is more plausible than the other, then such a study does not deserve to be referred to as a PhD at all. The idea of taking risks and playing off one risk against another is a philosophical action that accentuates a thinking-acting scenario. That is, any doctorate cannot be remiss of philosophical inquiry.

Any doctorate that does not consider whisper as sacrosanct can be considered a study that stands for some completed utopian product. It is as if the study claims to be the authoritative word on some scholarly matter and that nothing more can be said about it. This, I have argued, is an impossibility as there is always more to know and learn in what is still to come. And this means that any study cannot be exhausted. Even more devastating to know is that when students and supervisors do not engage in wandering, they stop thinking as humans about the work at hand. We all know this is impossible as humans always contemplate and reflect on their praxis. If thinking is aborted, then there is no point in pursuing a study as demanding as a doctorate that incessantly requires thinking beings. The point about reconsidering human reasonableness is not to abandon it but to look at it differently to come up with something unexpected and perhaps not thought of.

Doctorates without whispering are philosophically flawed texts. By and large, wonder, wander, and whisper are ethical actions that, if ignored in doctoral inquiries, would deprive such studies of ethical concerns. This would mean that doctorates would not have anything ethical to offer the public good. In this way, doctoral studies would be considered irrelevant writing without any philosophical and pragmatic appeal – that is, it is irrelevant to societal change.

What seems even more disconcerting about the philosophical dilemma that faces doctoral education in Southern Africa is that such studies would not be responsive to the many societal dystopias on the continent. If the dilemma of doctoral education is not recognised as a philosophical problem, how would it be possible to eradicate societal dystopias? Is it possible for doctoral studies to respond to undesirable situations on the continent if such studies are not appropriately conceptualised? I cannot see how a study on violence that has not been conceived and constructed according to credible lines of argument can be useful to practical dilemmas on the continent. Do we expect an ill-conceived study on violence to respond to gender-based violence and inequality, patriarchal dominance, and the persecution and torturing of women during civil strife on the African continent? So the predicament of being remiss of wonder, wander, and whisper during doctoral studies – philosophical negligence – is a betrayal of the real predicament of violence that continues unabatedly on the continent and needs to be quelled.

In the main, my argument is one in defence of philosophy, more specifically, the enactment of a philosophy of higher education on the African continent. Such an African philosophy of higher education would not only broaden our thinking in addressing dilemmas on the continent but invariably summon us to look at the ramifications of major societal problems for African higher education. More specifically, it would make us think differently about doctoral pursuits that seem largely about extrinsic gains at the moment but not about their responsiveness to dilemmas on the continent that stare us all in the eye. It is long overdue that we look more critically at doctoral studies that can respond to societal dilemmas on the continent, albeit at societal, environmental, economic, or political levels. But this would require a deepened form of doctoral education and supervision – one that seems commensurate with wonder, wander, and whisper. It needs philosophical repositioning.

Are doctoral studies still at risk?

I would respond in the affirmative for several reasons. Firstly, any doctoral study that does not take seriously notions of educational theory would not be able to enhance the study's credibility at all. An educational theory provides substantive insights into understandings in and about education. It constitutes meanings of education that have been examined and justified according to argumentation and debate. Thus, being remiss of educational theory, as several of the doctorates in higher education attest to, is a matter of risking the relevancy of such studies. Simply put, its relevance becomes questionable, considering that educational theory substantiates what has been examined rigorously. Secondly, a doctorate at risk does not offer responsiveness to societal and political issues. If doctorates cannot respond to societal issues and political education, higher education would remain in peril based on its dependence on the pertinence of such studies. How can higher education expand as a field of inquiry that needs to respond to issues in the sector if it does not provide possibilities to address societal and political issues? For instance, what does a philosophy of higher education have to offer institutional and structural changes in the sector if it has not been stretched? Thirdly, if doctoral education does not show the capacity to respond to ethical dilemmas, say on the African continent, it is very unlikely that such predicaments would abate. I am specifically thinking of issues of migration, inequalities, stereotyping, and the vilification of humans through conflict and wars. This would mean that doctoral studies are incapable of responding ethically to predicaments on the continent and, by implication, will be at risk of vanishing into oblivion.

In the main, higher education institutions cannot allow their doctoral programmes and initiatives to succumb to irrelevance and uselessness, for that would mean that the higher education sector has become futile – a situation Southern African higher education institutions can ill-afford to let happen. The next section addresses how a decolonised doctoral programme at an *ubuntu* university can unfold.

Towards a decolonised doctoral education programme

As mentioned elsewhere, colonisation is a fractured approach to human living whereby dominant groups consider it acceptable to impose their ways of living and being on subjugated others, taking away others' legitimate rights to decide for themselves (Waghid et al., 2018). Decolonising higher education attempts to rupture the controlling actions of others and foreground the less-dominant people's cultural, political, intellectual, and moral ways of being. In this way, a decolonised doctoral education programme aims to rupture higher educational discourse whereby teachers and students first take the initiative to think and act for themselves in resistance to being told what to do. This means that when students apply for access to a particular doctoral education programme at an *ubuntu* university, these students should inform faculty what they intend to study in a particular doctoral educational programme and not always what they will be told to do. Put differently, students decide on the curriculum they intend to embark on – that is, they become the initiators of their doctoral pursuits. This makes sense because if students initiate the curriculum – intellectual judgements, critical thinking, ethical actions, democratic engagements (Pinar, 2004) – that should constitute it, they become the intersubjective agents of curriculum inquiry so necessary for a transformative decolonised educational approach.

Secondly, a decolonised doctoral education curriculum requires that teachers and students become self-reflexive beings whereby they develop a desire to look at things anew – that is, recognise that they have something else to offer by wedging their critical voice into higher education. And for this to happen, students should enter a doctoral education programme with their preferred texts that could hopefully contribute to their empowered positions as critical and responsible teachers and learners. For example, as exceptionally highly valued texts in and about the decolonisation of higher education studies, I would welcome the works of established decolonial scholars like N'Dri Assiè-Lumumba (2005), Walter Mignolo (2010), and Achille Mbembe (2012).

Thirdly, a decolonised view of doctoral education involves looking differently at the notion of democratic citizenship education. We integrate a notion of *ubuntu* within such a notion of education and then analyse how such an understanding of education has been altered. Of course, having done extensive work on the idea of what constitutes an *ubuntu* university (Waghid et al., 2023), we reconceptualise decolonised higher education based on a notion of *ubuntu* according to which autonomous action, iteration, and co-responsibility seem to emerge as constitutive notions of such a form of education. Thus, fusing indigenous or local understandings of concepts with established democratic practices is one way of interconnecting the local with the global, giving rise to a glocalised understanding of human action.

Fourthly, students are encouraged to embark on dissent throughout their doctoral writing. They need to subvert the taken-for-granted understandings of concepts and practices to show that offering resistance as an act of decolonisation can lead to more nuanced interpretations of ideas espoused in their theses. I encourage students to look differently at concepts, in particular, showing how higher pedagogy can be altered.

Fifthly, I urge students to reconsider the notion of decolonised cosmopolitan education that allows individuals to look at others without misrecognising them or trying to impose their understanding of concepts on others. To act in a cosmopolitan way, students are encouraged to recognise people for who they are and not what we want them to be. The idea of cosmopolitan education is connected to the exercise of respect towards what is other and different and without opposing diversity of views and perspectives.

Sixthly, decolonised doctoral education should advance a notion of epistemic justice that recognises equality among supervisors and students pertaining to their knowledge claims (Fricker, 2007). When supervisors and students treat one another equally, such relations oppose opportunities for exclusion, marginalisation, and domination. When such a form of equal doctoral supervision occurs, the plausibility of theses would be enhanced.

Summary

Doctoral supervision is both a rigorous and gratifying experience. As a rigorous activity, supervisors are expected to offer prescient comments on students' work. There is no point in supervising students without any feedback that would enhance the writing of students. Similarly, the expectation should always be that students respond to the comments offered by supervisors, as that would be a way of honouring the arduous work done by supervisors. I cannot imagine students ignoring supervisors' insights into their theses without responding adequately to such concerns raised. It is somewhat thoughtful to consider supervisors' comments before being informed by examiners of similar matters identified by vigilant supervisors. Equally, doctoral examinations can be very gratifying. It is gratifying when reputable examiners comment on students' work. These examiners are discerning and esteemed in their fields of inquiry, and taking their advice is highly honourable for students and supervisors. I take tremendous pleasure in submitting our students' doctoral work to such examiners as I am convinced that reputable scholars treat others' doctoral work with the dignity and respect it deserves. If this happens, doctoral education would no longer be at risk.

References

Assiè-Lumumba, N. T. (2005). African higher education: From compulsory juxtaposition to fusion by choice – forging a new philosophy of education for social progress. In Y. Waghid (Ed.), *African(a) philosophy of education: Reconstructions and deconstructions* (pp. 19–53). Department of Education Policy Studies.

Cloete, N., Mouton, J., & Sheppard, G. (2015). *Doctoral education in South Africa: Policy, discourse, and data*. African Minds.

Council on Higher Education. (2022). *Doctoral degrees national report*. CHE Press.

Derrida, J. (2004). *Eyes of the university: Right to philosophy 2* (J Plug et al., Trans.). Stanford University Press.

Fricker, M. (2007). *Epistemic injustice: Power and the ethics of knowing*. Oxford University Press.

Herman, C. (2017). Looking back at doctoral education in South Africa. *Studies in Higher Education, 42*(8), 1437–1454.

Mbembe, A. (2012). Decolonizing the university: New directions. *Arts and Humanities in Higher Education, 15*(1), 29–45. https://doi.org/10.1177/1474022215618513

Mignolo, W. D. (2010). Epistemic disobedience, independent thought and decolonial freedom. *Theory, Culture and Society, 26*(7–8), 159–181. https://doi.org/10.1177/0263276409349275

Pinar, W. F. (2004). *What is curriculum theory?* Lawrence Erlbaum.

Waghid, Y., Terblanche, J., Shawa, L., Hungwe, J., Waghid, F., & Waghid, Z. (2023). *Towards an ubuntu university: African higher education reimagined*. Palgrave Macmillan.

Waghid, Y., Waghid, F., & Waghid, Z. (2018). *Rupturing African philosophy on teaching and learning: Ubuntu justice and education*. Palgrave Macmillan.

Afterword
A personal reflection on conditioned thought

Introduction

I have decided to draw this book to a conclusion in reference to a reflective moment because I would reiterate my primary reason for engaging with the notion of a decolonised African higher education agenda. Giving thought to doctoral education means that one must understand what goes on inside the practice and have an idea of what happens outside of it. To say something has an inside is an acknowledgement that there are certain things without which the concept cannot be without. These aspects or features make a concept or practice what it is. To get an idea of those aspects of a concept that constitute it, reflect on what is inside the concept. Doctoral education is what it is because what students research and articulate based on their engagements with texts and supervisors makes the practice what it is – its inside. What lies outside of the practice – its periphery – is how the concept manifests in practices. So doctoral education consists of an outside whereby students and supervisors act in such a way that they point out how doctoral education enhances a transformative or decolonial agenda of higher education. Thus, reflecting on doctoral education, including supervision, implies that one has something to say about how the concept of doctoral education manifests in actions by students. The narratives that follow provide accounts of how doctoral education is experienced by others as both insiders and outsiders.

On having read Grant Farred's (2020) *Derrida and Africa: Jacques Derrida as a Figure for African Thought*, I thought about my own academic work as an African scholar who has come to respect many of the thoughts of Derrida, particularly on deconstruction, reason (thought), the university, becoming, and cosmopolitanism. Undoubtedly, I often used Derrida to make sense of higher educational challenges and complexities in Africa. What attracted me most to his work is that thought about the other is always conditioned to be beyond one's grasp – that is, 'conditioned of being beyond reach' (Martinon, 2020, p. 89). I concur with the latter Derridian perspective as I invariably encountered my students (the other) as beyond reach. This means that I was not always capable of grasping them fully, as some of their expressions could be conceived as having been beyond my reach. I have tried to make sense of my students' work, so I have always acknowledged their writing. But like Derrida, I would argue that paradoxically, there have been moments in their writing where their alterity has not been identified or secured. Of course, this experience might not be conditioned upon my lack of understanding of their work, which would be tantamount to disrespecting their writing. Rather, it is an acknowledgement that the other should be left unconditioned (with her own independence of thought) and not be conditioned according to what I had in mind for them. In this Derridian way, I retained respect towards my students and their writings. Yet I would not posit that all of my writings and supervision embody a Derridian approach to philosophy and the philosophy of higher education.

Before I earnestly started reading Derrida in the early 2000s, I was already immersed in thought about academic work 'without determination' (Martinon, 2020, p. 88). In other words, when I thought about notions of democracy, citizenship, and education just after the completion of my doctorate in the 1990s, I was engaged with thoughts 'that had no pre-determined end in sight' (Martinon, 2020, p. 88). For me, thought was always an act of wandering without envisaging some fixed perspective in and about a notion of democratic citizenship education. Consequently, I always encouraged my students to begin their doctoral work with some understanding that they would expand on the concept and even come up with something not thought about previously. There was no predetermined end in sight with where our thoughts on democratic citizenship education might take us. Paradoxically speaking, it is a form of conditioned thought that encourages us to look at things unconditionally. How academics and students become conditioned by thoughts that will take them towards the unconditioned, unexpected, and improbable can vary. It can happen by reading a text, engaging with someone, or watching a play or movie. My conditioning towards the unconditioned occurred as a consequence of my reading of the Quran – a text prescribed to that intent on gaining closeness to a higher good. It is to such a discussion that I now turn.

On being conditioned by Quranic expressions: in the quest for meaning

The Quran is a voluminous text comprising 30 parts (juz pl. *adjzā'*) and 114 chapters (*sūrah pl. suwar*). It is described as a book of guidance for those who believe in Allāh Almighty, His angels, revealed books, prophets, the eschatological life, and the prevalence of good and bad in this life, which Allāh is all aware of. I was conditioned with the thought that the Quran is my guiding text, which should be memorised, read, interpreted, and practised in my daily life. As my grandfather was my mentor, he emphasised that living a life based on the Quran would invariably secure my passage to paradise. Consequently, I found myself engaging with the Quran from a very tender age:

reciting it eloquently, reading it with insight, and attempting to live according to its guidance for most of my life. Of course, no human is infallible, and I would be the last one to claim that I have always lived my life based on every piece of guidance the Quran advocates. However, I have tried to live decently, respectfully, and thoughtfully.

There is one particular verse that profoundly impacted me since I have encountered and re-read it many times and which conditioned my thoughts about life, humans, and engagement with others. In relation to *Sūrah al-Ḥujurāt* – the Apartments (chapter 49: verse 13), of the Holy Quran, the concept of *ta'arruf* can be elucidated in the following ways: Firstly, humankind is summoned to engage in *ta'arruf* (associational knowing) – that is, to associate with all other humans. The concept of *ta'arruf* is derived from the Arabic root, '*arafa*, which literally means 'to know'. About '*arafa*, a prominent *Ḥadīth* (Prophetic saying) explains the verb as follows: 'Whoever knows himself [herself] knows his [her] Lord'. The idea of knowing the self is linked to the notion that humans have autonomous selves. In a way, being invited to engage with the autonomous or independent self is a precondition for acquiring a sense of spiritualism – that is, getting to know a sense of the Being responsible for the self's existence. Yet the most poignant moment in the elucidation of '*arafa* – to know – is a matter of exercising one's efforts in coming to understand one's autonomous self (*nafs*). Put differently, one's understanding of one's autonomous self would most appropriately awaken the relations one is about to engage in with others – a matter of committing oneself to a renewed possibility of engagement. Thus, in relation to human interactions, the notion of *ta'arruf* is conditional upon getting to know the autonomous self and its capabilities. This is necessary for whatever the nature of encounters and the autonomous self envisages engaging in. However, what seems evident from the *Ḥadīth* given earlier is that an earnest commitment to come to know the self is inextricably connected to a knowledge of the Lord – that is, the One who educates (*rabb*).

One of the most salient aspects in understanding Allāh's names or references to His being is that humans should aspire to become like what His names represent. Of course, I am not intimating the impossibility of humans ever becoming like Allāh. Rather, I am accentuating the claim that if the Divine Being introduces Himself as, for instance, *al-Raḥmān* (the Compassionate) and *al-Raḥīm* (the One who forgives), then the implication is that humans should become compassionate and forgiving considering that they commit themselves to engaging with Allāh's creation, more specifically other humans. Of course, it is impossible that humans will ever become anything near Allāh, but it seems quite possible for humans to act compassionately and forgivingly – that is, humanely. What follows is that any human aspiration should be accompanied by autonomy to mould the self according to Allāh Almighty's all-encompassing descriptions – an important facet of any form of associational knowing. When humans act autonomously, they not only strive to become Allāh-conscious but also emulate the qualities of Allāh so that their interactions with other humans would be pursued along the lines of virtues associated with reverential actions. By implication, *ta'arruf* (associational knowing) implies that human autonomy should be enacted according to virtues that enhance respectful human engagement. Put differently, human encounters are not constituted only by what humans conceive to be rational but also emotional and spiritual, such as divulging through virtuous devotion.

The significance of educating humans is the devout virtues of *ghufrān* (forgiveness) and *raḥmah* (compassion). And, if autonomous human action were to be enacted, then such action should be guided by what it means to forgive and be compassionate. The point is that autonomous human action is conditional upon enacting virtues associated with some higher transcendental good (Allāh-consciousness). And, if *ta'arruf* (associational knowing) manifests in human practices, then autonomous action must have been guided by virtues of devotion and compassion for one another – that is, in an individual's relations with all others.

Secondly, engaging in *ta'arruf* (associational knowing) is also conditional upon encountering others different from oneself – that is, a movement towards an other. Engaging with different others is already a recognition that humanity does not comprise monocultural individuals and communities. That *ta'arruf* (associational knowing) is constituted by recognising that humanity comprises pluricultural communities is a vindication that different others are invited to encounter one another with their diverse perspectives and otherness. If not, what would be the point of embarking on such encounters? When different people come together, they might agree and find consensus or alternatively disagree and achieve dissensus. The latter is so because human encounters are modes of action that bring people intersubjectively into communication with one another with the possibility that they may or may not find common ground.

Of importance to the notion of *ta'arruf* (associational knowing) is an understanding that humans have to engage so that they encounter one another, and what ensues can be that they learn from their engagement based on *shūrā* (mutual consultation). Yet learning from one another based on *shūrā* implies that humans should engage in deliberation with one another. That is, engagement should be subjected to one another's articulations. If not, there would not be the possibility that people would listen to one another. Listening is an important facet of *shūrā* (mutual consultation) because one gets an opportunity to experience what the other has to say. Without listening, there cannot be any *shūrā* (mutual consultation), and the possibility of *ta'arruf* (associational knowing) would be unnecessarily constrained. The point about *shūrā* (mutual consultation) is that humans are summoned to engage with one another. And engaging with one another implies that humans express their points of view and even show a willingness to listen to what the other has to say. If articulation and listening do not manifest, we cannot legitimately talk about *shūrā* (mutual consultation). By implication, *shūrā* (mutual consultation) is conditional upon articulation and listening. However, listening seems to be accentuated within the practice of *shūrā* (mutual consultation) because listening gives the other and one an opportunity to take what has been heard into some kind of scrutiny and, hence, talk back to what has been heard. If there is no talking back to the points articulated and listened to, there would be an absence of legitimate *shūrā* (mutual consultation). What is the point of articulating oneself, listening to others, and never critically examining the thoughts of others and letting others know about one's analyses of their views? In such a case, *shūrā* (mutual consultation) would not happen as the practice is conditional upon articulation, listening, and talking back. This is what is meant by engaging with one another. Reserving the right not to talk back would render any *shūrā* (mutual consultation) and, by implication, *ta'arruf* (associational knowing) untenable. In any human encounter, justifiable speech through argumentation and wise words should be prevalent when an educational discourse is at stake. In other words, *ta'arruf* (associational knowing) can never be coupled with forms of hostility that alienate (exclude) humans from encounters rather than keeping in touch with them through justifiable speech. And here, wise and just speech is a vindication that any summoning of people (*da'wah*) cannot be linked to coercion as that in itself would undermine the free and willing acts of human engagement that constitute the notion of *ta'arruf* (associational knowing). If human encounters are not free and autonomous, the possibility is always there that humans might be excluded from the encounter based on humiliation and belligerence. What makes *ta'arruf* (associational knowing) a legitimate summoning of people to engage in encounters is that such encounters are not intended to exclude humans and that justifiable speech would be used to summon them to engage with one another.

Thirdly, in reference to the opening expression of *Sūrah al-Ḥujurāt* – the Apartments (chapter 49: verse 13), '*yā ayyuha al-nās* – verily, humankind!', it is evident that humans are summoned to engage in encounters. Now, the rationale for cultivating humanity is premised on the practice of *ta'arruf* (associational knowing). Humans are not just summoned to engage with one another. Rather the potentiality of human encounters is geared towards the cultivation of humanity. And this implies that humans should engage with one another based on civility and deliberative speech. If not, how would it ever be possible that they might learn from one another? More specifically, how is it possible to initiate new thoughts or breakthroughs? Cultivating humanity is espoused quite succinctly in the *Qurān* in *Sūrah Fuṣṣilat* (chapter 41: verse 33): 'Who is better in speech than one who calls (men) to *Allāh*, works righteousness, and says "I am of those who bow in Islam"?'

Being Muslim in submission to Allāh Almighty is associated with performing righteous acts in service of Allāh and His creations. Thus, cultivating humanity in relation to acting righteously – that is, devoutly and justly – is synonymous with being Muslim or one who surrenders to Allāh Almighty. By

Afterword 81

implication, when humans encounter one another, they commit themselves to act righteously; otherwise, they would not be cultivating humanity. As aptly reminded in the *Qurān* in *Sūrah Āli 'Imrān* – the Family of Amran (Ali, 1922): 'Let there arise out of you a band of people inviting all that is good, enjoining what is right, and forbidding what is wrong; they are the ones to attain felicity'. Of importance here is the emphasis the *Qurān* places on becoming those who flourish – that is, the *muflihūn*. This community of flourishing beings would invariably summon one another to goodness and announce themselves with just as opposed to unjust action. What is also significant about cultivating humanity through *ta'arruf* (associational knowing) is that every individual is also summoned to take stock of himself or herself concerning cultivating humanity. As the Qurān states in *Sūrah al-Ḥashr* – the Banishment (chapter 59: verse 18): 'O you who believe! Fear *Allāh* and let every soul look to what (provision) he has sent forth for the morrow. And fear *Allāh*: for *Allāh* is well-acquainted with (all) that you do'.

The point about being cognisant of the human self is linked to the practice of being open and reflective about the self and the traditions to which one might be attached. In this way, one would remain open and reflective about one's own cultural-religious attachments. Put differently, working towards cultivating humanity cannot be enacted without looking at the autonomous self and how the self is situated and guided by the traditions to which the self is attached. It is not possible to cultivate humanity if one does not look independently at one's self. It was narrated by Caliph 'Umar that people need to take stock of themselves – openly reflect on themselves – in preparation for Judgement Day, a vindication that openly reflecting on the self is necessary for cultivating humanity. Hence, two aspects emanate from understanding why and how one contributes towards cultivating humanity: firstly, to be reflective and open about the self; and secondly, to be open and reflective towards that which is in becoming. In these ways, one's encounters with others will possibly be enhanced. That is, *ta'arruf* (associational knowing) is inextricably connected to the self being reflectively open to his or her own attachments – traditions, cultures, ethnicities, and ways of being and ways of acting – and, concomitantly with self-reflection, the self remains open to that which is still in becoming.

Thus far, I have argued, firstly, why the practice of *ta'arruf* (associational knowing) is conditional upon getting to know the autonomous self and its capabilities. Secondly, *ta'arruf* (associational knowing) involves summoning different people to engage in deliberative encounters that can result in justifiable speech. That is, there always seems to be a leaning towards the other. Thirdly, *ta'arruf* (associational knowing) is inextricably connected to the self being reflectively open about the self and its attachments; concomitantly being open and reflective towards what remains in becoming – a matter of being open to new thoughts. In the above ways, *ta'arruf* (associational knowing) has the potential to cultivate humanity. Cultivating humanity is not just about being concerned about one's ways of acting and doing but extending one's internal openness and reflectiveness to others. Only then would one's encounters with others be legitimate as one does not engage with others on the basis of prejudice towards one's own ways of being and acting. The way one has been reared and learnt through one's upbringing influences one's relations with others. I now move on to a discussion related to cultivating humanity.

Cultivating humanity amidst African challenges of inequality, unfreedom, and injustice through doctoral supervision

My engagement with the Quranic text conditioned my thought about human and non-human life based on a notion of associational knowing (*ta'arruf*). Any exposure to new thoughts happens because of one's engagement with others and otherness. Likewise, engaging with others and otherness enhances the possibility of deliberative engagement based on which humans can collectively work against forms of injustice they might experience or become exposed to. In this way, I always provoked my students to think anew about the inequalities, injustices and inhumanities faced by people on the African continent and elsewhere. Unsurprisingly, all my doctoral students related their work to resisting injustice, unfreedom, inequality, and inhumanity on the African continent, specifically matters pertaining to higher education in Southern Africa. Thus, a supervisor's own experiences might influence students' work. And considering that my work mostly deals with decolonial ventures in higher education, my students' work gained more potentiality when based on some of the higher education matters I engaged with.

By far, the most significant doctoral projects I supervised dealt with a conditioned idea of critical thought whereby students could act autonomously and deliberatively with texts with the aim of bringing about freedom and emancipation through their work. Yet the outcomes of the doctoral contributions were left to the unconditioned possibilities – that is, unexpected and improbable moments that might yet ensue from their work. For instance, one is yet to see the possible consequences of a radical cosmopolitanism for higher education in Southern Africa, how a renewed form of critical pedagogy will guide teacher education in Southern African universities, or how decolonised communitarianism might influence institutional autonomy at Southern African universities. Such has been the thrust of my supervisory acts and my approach to doctoral education studies for the last three decades. I hope to continue on this path of getting to know the other in their otherness, embarking upon deliberative engagement with students, and continuing on a path of supervision where doctoral outcomes remain narratives in becoming.

Furthermore, with an avalanche of academic and non-academic texts on the use of educational technology in university education, I want to pause and reflect on what it means for doctoral supervision. I now highlight three reflective moments on the use of educational technology in higher education: Google Scholar, ChatGPT, and a metaphor of rhythm. I now show how the latter impacts my thinking related to doctoral supervision.

Google Scholar as a matrix for theoretical adventures

I received a message from Donatello that he wished to pursue a doctoral degree under my supervision. I have never met him before and relied on his CV to acquaint myself with his academic background. I then requested that he send me some tentative thoughts on the topic he envisages investigating – usually around 2,000 words. The expectation was that he would immerse himself in an independent study and begin to think immediately about his research project. I instantly encouraged Donatello to continue with his studies without questioning his motives for doing so. I then heard him whisper in my ears: Can you not provide me with sources about the topic I am pursuing? I urged Donatello to do a Google Scholar search about the theme his research involves. Let's say it was about educational technology and democratic education. To my excitement, Donatello came up with several sources, including academic articles and books on the topic. He was then requested to provide analytical summaries of the work he identified and how the theoretical ideas potentially impact his research. In a way, his literature review or analysis was produced. He then had to show how his theoretical analysis informed his topic and what the potential gaps were in the work he is now knowledgeable about. Once a student is acquainted with the literature on his topic, he could easily grasp how his work could be guided. Google scholar searches enable students to gain access to their fields of inquiry, particularly when they use highly rated journals in the fields.

ChatGPT as my philosophical interlocutor

The artificial intelligence programme, ChatGPT, can be used to ascertain what prominent scholars have to say about one's topic of investigation. At least, one would come to know and corroborate what theoretical insights already exist in and about one's topic of investigation. For example, if a student wants to know what the main arguments on democratic education of, say, Gert Biesta – a prominent educational philosopher – are, then ChatGPT can be used to solicit such narratives. Students would then have to make sense of what has been written by the author and be spurred into action to read the actual seminal works of the author on the topic. Just duplicating what ChatGPT says about the author would be tantamount to plagiarism. However, gaining ideas about the author's seminal works and articulating one's own understanding of such work invariably subvert plagiarism.

Desert adventures as a metaphor for doctoral pursuits

To think of one's doctoral work as a metaphorical drive through the desert with one's 4 × 4 vehicle, speeding up and down the sand dunes, reminds one of a rhythmic approach to doctoral studies. The act of driving through a desert is already a demanding task in the sense that one has to remain vigilant about not overturning one's vehicle. In the same way, a doctoral thesis has to be steered with some accuracy and determination; otherwise one might not enjoy the study. The metaphor of rhythm is a recognition that, at times, one's writing is clear and substantiated. But other times it might not be as organised and argumentative, meaning one should suspend one's writing momentarily. Once one has thought through one's articulations, one can re-enter the fold of writing to produce more systematic and substantive pieces of writing. In other words, holding back with the intention to advance in one's writing is a matter of writing rhythmically (Agamben, 1999). Rhythmic writing is especially necessary when students connect their theoretical analyses with findings of their research. Rhythmic writing thus assists students to produce more coherent and theoretically informed texts.

Thus, I have shown how Google Scholar, ChatGPT, and the metaphor of rhythm can expedite thesis writing. Google Scholar enables students to access significant works about the field of inquiry, whereby theoretical positioning can be enhanced. ChatGPT could foreground deep analytical reflections of major scholars' work that could be used to substantiate students' claims about educational matters. And the action of rhythm bears considerable fruit on authors' texts in substantive and well-grounded ways. Next, I finally look at how I was conditioned to think about African (philosophy) of education in the context of *ubuntu* and doctoral work.

Enhancing *ubuntu* education: doctoral encounters reconsidered

The argument of this final section is premised on the idea that doctoral encounters will be much more tenable if reconsidered in light of rethinking a notion of the African ethic of *ubuntu*. Literally, *ubuntu*, designated with different terms in the various languages across the continent, is in substance pronounced in African parlance as human dignity and interdependence through the dictum 'I am because we are'; more specifically, a person is only so on the basis of her association with other persons: *ubuntu ngumuntu ngabanye abantu*. My argument is threefold: Firstly, education, like *ubuntu*, ought to denote a human encounter in which people confront one another through agreement, dissent, resistance, and/or cooperation. Secondly, education, like *ubuntu*, should be underscored by acts of openness and reflexivity through which people present themselves and, by implication, their situations in moments of critique and iteration, although in practice it has reflected at times in an unequal world that denies the premise of equality (Waghid, 2014). Thirdly, my argument for a renewed understanding of *ubuntu*, and hence education, is one that is closely drawn to the notion that, like any form of education, encounters with its concomitant links with *ubuntu* can never be finalised. Rather, it remains in becoming as it continuously evolves towards what seems improbable and unimaginable, though the challenges of the world call for its application. Thus, by making sense of a reconsidered view of *ubuntu*, I have to offer another perspective of education – that is, a human encounter in which reflexivity, critique, and iteration hold sway to advance what such a discourse of education cultivates.

Education, like other forms of education, albeit philosophy of education, history of education, sociology of education, or psychology of education, is constituted by a rationale that makes such a form of education what it is. Implicit in an understanding of education as discourse, I affirm the paradigm of thinking that underscores my understanding of education. The very idea of conceiving education as discourse is in line with Foucault's notion that discourse is a human practice (Foucault, 1972). In much the same way Michel Foucault construed understandings of knowledge in the context of social practices constituted by human subjectivities and relations of power, I consider education as a human practice guided by subjectivities and power relations. Firstly, considering that education is a form of action that relies on human interpretation, its meanings are guided by the subjectivities of humans. Put differently, we would not be practising education devoid of our subjective reflections on its meanings – a matter of how education can be conceived as a discourse. Secondly, like any form of education, education is grounded in a deliberative discourse – that is, an encounter – of human engagement and iteration. There cannot be any talk of education without the human practice of engagement and iteration, more specifically, the practice of human deliberation about that which makes education a discourse. When iterative action manifests in the pursuit of education, humans bring multiple understandings of knowledge into a conversation. Through a rupturing of thought, sudden upheavals of human thinking emerge in which meanings of education are foregrounded. Thirdly, education as discourse also lays bare possibilities of the practice one might not have thought of before to the extent that the unpredictable and unexpected might arise. The mere fact that education is practised by humans means the possibility is always there that unforeseen possibilities might ensue as a discourse – that is, possibilities that might surface unexpectedly without necessarily any predictive element involved. In the main, education is a discourse constituted by the agency of human subjectivity, iterative human action, and the relentless pursuit of unforeseen possibilities. If education as discourse were to manifest, the possibility is always there that it might resonate with the practice of *ubuntu* on the grounds that both practices – education and *ubuntu* – hold the potential for agreement and dissensus. In this way, talking about education as an act of *ubuntu* would not be inappropriate.

The conceptual connection between education as discourse and *ubuntu* rests on the view that both concepts are human actions intertwined with an iterative concern towards otherness and difference. Looking at education as a discourse of *ubuntu*, one instantaneously reifies the practice of human subjectivity, particularly the quest for subjective meanings. When human subjectivities are summoned to come to speech, the possibility is always there for people to engage in deliberation about public matters. For example, public deliberation is often required to resolve matters pertaining to socio-political challenges that confront humans such as poverty and hunger, inequality and unemployment, racial discrimination and exclusion, domestic abuse, violence against women, and other forms of gender inequality. The point I am making is that unless public deliberation on contentious matters gains the required attention we would not be doing education and, by implication, would be remiss of enacting *ubuntu*. When education is enacted as discourse, humans are summoned to engage in public deliberation with the possibility that they can agree on controversial matters. If an agreement is not imminent, there is no harm in reaching a disagreement or dissensus. The French philosopher, Jacques Rancière (2011, p. 10), offers an account of dissensus whereby humans put matters into question without unravelling matters of public and domestic concern in their entirety. Through dissensus, thinking unfolds through which 'the wrong that cannot be settled . . . can be processed all the time' (Rancière, 2011, p. 11). Put differently, practising a critique of dissensus involves tracing back understandings of a concept and, concurrently, looking for descriptions, narrations, metaphors, and symbols that constitute such concepts. Thus, a Rancièrean account of doing education would involve a critique of dissensus and unsettlement. Now when education is guided by an act of dissensus, then such a form of action requires one to not only look at what lies outside of the practice but also explore what it means to look inside of education – an idea that invariably invokes the notion of *ubuntu*.

When one looks at what education entails if ruptured from the inside, one bears testimony to what makes it what it is. Giorgio Agamben (2002) offers an account of witnessing in which humans bear testimony to pronouncements of events and human experiences from the inside. Simply put, through dissensus, witnessing becomes possible from the inside – that is, on account of a person's own experiences concerning acts of torment, suffering, and horror – inhumane experiences that seem to undermine education itself (Agamben, 2002, p. 45). In other words, education constituted by the testimony of witnessing involves rupturing those unjust and inhumane acts associated with coloniality, gender discrimination, exclusion, and other forms of democratic injustice. Considering that many of the constraints and restrictions experienced in educational institutions today actually come from within the institutions themselves, an education of dissensus and, by implication, witnessing would be fearless of inhumanity and democratic injustice, especially when these come from the inside. Amy Gutmann (2003) aptly reminds us that questioning from inside

Afterword   87

is synonymous with being open-minded and exercising dissent. Yet open-mindedness and dissent are important ways a democratic citizenry exercises democratic justice: civic equality, equal freedom, and opportunity for all (Gutmann, 2003, p. 209). And, considering that democratic justice cannot be exercised without a deep commitment to dissensus, witnessing, and critical questioning, it follows that a democratic citizenry cannot do without a deep ethical commitment to act freely (autonomously) and non-discriminately (Gutmann, 2003). In this way, acting with critique on the basis of dissensus and witnessing, education invariably draws on acts of *ubuntu* – that is, those acts of virtue that allow humans to act with dignity, humanity, and democratic justice (Waghid, 2014). If education were to be constituted by notions of agreement and dissensus, the possibility is always there for virtues of *ubuntu* to manifest in human encounters. Thus, education as an act of (dis)agreement creates conditions for the enactment of *ubuntu* on the grounds of which human encounters in social and institutional practices would be non-repressive, non-discriminatory, and humane. Next, I examine how such acts of *ubuntu* contribute to education's distinctively cosmopolitan outlook.

I now offer an account of David T. Hansen's (2011) take on cosmopolitan education, particularly how it is commensurate with *ubuntu*. Thereafter, I show what education would look like if organised according to a cosmopolitan framework of *ubuntu*. For Hansen (2011, p. 113), cosmopolitanism in education is constituted by a 'reflective openness to the new and reflective loyalty to the known'. Being cosmopolitan is connected with the human subjectivity of reflection. When comparative educationists reflect, they come together to engage reciprocally about their knowledge and understanding of self, others, and the world (Hansen, 2011, p. 9). When they do so, they reflect on the unknown and equally reflect on what is known and familiar. Cosmopolitan-mindedness involves being reflective about that which is held in high esteem by one and not to blindly accept all of the new unknown without first evaluating it. In this way, cosmopolitan-minded comparative educationists are able to remain rooted in their identities while, at the same time, they are open to being transformed through that which is new or in becoming (Hansen, 2011). Thus, comparative educationists who act in a cosmopolitan way are reflective of what they do. Likewise, they also show a 'reflective openness' in their encounters with others, whereby they commit themselves to learn from them (Hansen, 2011, p. 60). Openness in such a manner is inextricably connected to virtues of *ubuntu*, such as being generous and hospitable in relations with others (Hansen, 2011).

Also, enacting cosmopolitanism through education is concomitantly linked to the cultivation of justice for all of humanity (Hansen, 2011, p. 33). Here I have in mind the cosmopolitan task of education to enhance change in the lived realities of the marginalised and often excluded. With its intent to cultivate justice for all humans, education advances a cosmopolitan ethos that can alleviate the exclusion of the other. In this way, a cosmopolitan take on education is tantamount to acting with discernment and an appreciation of the ways of others that might be incommensurable with one's own ways of being and acting. In other words, education has an inherent concern to undermine and transcend prejudices towards otherness and difference with a recognition that there is always more to learn through one's engagements with others. In this way, education has a disruptive potential in the sense that it undermines unequal, discriminatory, and prejudiced human constructions and interactions.

What follows from such a cosmopolitan demand for reflection is that educationists are obliged to proffer judgements on the claims people hold (Hansen, 2011). And, if such claims are homophobic, xenophobic, Islamophobic, anti-Semitic, racist, sexist, and dismissive, then education is required to proffer counter-judgements to deal with injurious modes of human action. Hansen (2011) introduces an important aspect pertaining to the enhancement of cosmopolitan education by positing that 'cosmopolitan-minded education assists people in moving closer and closer apart and further and further together' (Hansen, 2011, p. 3). When humans begin to know one another more intimately, it is possible to recognise more clearly than before why the self and the other are distinctly different from one another. Although the self and others might have gained a better understanding and appreciation of one another, they have become more aware perhaps of the disparities that continue to exist among them – a matter of moving closer apart. Likewise, humans, through their shared educational experiences, might enjoy time and space together, yet, by getting more acquainted with one another, there is always the possibility that the self and others might actually move further together (Hansen, 2011, p. 3). That is, they might be apart pragmatically but in reality, they share common understandings of perhaps exclusion, subjugation, and discrimination.

Considering that *ubuntu* is concerned with cultivating human values, such as those associated with harnessing one's humanity and expanding social engagements, it would not be inappropriate to assert that *ubuntu* seems to be a manifestation of education. In other words, an *ubuntu* take on education brings out the cosmopolitan acts of being engaged and responsive because humans are required not just to listen to others but rather 'listening with them' (Hansen, 2011, p. 116, our italics). The difference between listening to and listening with can be conceived as the difference between tolerating the other and being willing to be shaped by the other.

Hansen (2011, p. 166) avers that listening with others can be 'an imaginative, aesthetic exercise of trying to see the world as they do . . . to grasp the underlying values, beliefs, and aspirations that inform their ways of looking and knowing'. Listening with others requires, firstly, a particular willingness of the self to be open in the deliberative encounter with the other. Secondly, listening with others requires evaluating the unknown and determining what new perspectives should be allowed to influence one. This implies that a particular sense of judgement should be cultivated through (comparative) education. Hansen (2011) posits that one of the aims of education should be to engender in proponents of such a form of action capacities to cast judgements open to renewal with others (Hansen, 2011). When education is guided by an *ubuntu* notion of listening with others, cultivating humaneness in the self and the other would be highly possible. This practice of listening with others can inspire comparative educationists to become future problem-solvers and ethical agents of moral and societal change. Now that I have given some thought to the notion of a cosmopolitan education and its interconnectedness to *ubuntu* as listening with others, we move on to a discussion of how a renewed view of *ubuntu* can positively influence the form comparative education should assume.

I now argue why *ubuntu*, literally meaning human dignity and interdependence, is an appropriate practice to advocate for a renewed understanding of doctoral education. In revisiting some of my previous elucidations of *ubuntu*, three aspects come to mind: Firstly, *ubuntu* is connected to the notion of communitarian action; secondly, *ubuntu* has a profound cosmopolitan dimension; and thirdly, *ubuntu* has a strong human flourishing perspective (Waghid, 2014). I now briefly expand on these claims of *ubuntu*.

The renowned African philosopher, Kwasi Wiredu (2000, p. 374), posited that in traditional African society, people freely discussed with the elders sitting under big trees until they found agreement. This suggests that collective decision-making was recognised in traditional African communities to the extent that it was not difficult for many nation-states on the continent to recognise the significance of democratic politics. Now considering that collective decision-making and political agreement constituted the politico-social activities of traditional African societies, it can only be concluded that *ubuntu* – humanness and co-existence – was already part of the societal practices of Africa's populations (Waghid, 2014, p. 57). In this sense, firstly, *ubuntu*, as a communitarian human practice, was already pervasive among African communities to the extent that the Ghanaian scholar Kwame Gyekye (1997, p. 158) posits that the practice 'is a pervasive and fundamental [humanistic] concept in African socioethical thought generally – a concept that animates other intellectual activities, and forms of behaviour, including religious behaviour, and provides continuity, resilience, nourishment, and meaning of life'. Thus, *ubuntu* came to be associated with a communitarian understanding of human action – that is, as aptly stated in the African isiXhosa language in general discussions, *ubuntu ngumuntu ngabanye abantu* – a person is only a person through other persons (Waghid, 2014, p. 57).

What is significant in an exposition on *ubuntu* is that individual autonomy is not abandoned for the sake of community. Rather, community is enacted through the autonomous actions of individuals. This idea seems commensurable with Frederick Nietzsche's call for self-reflective individuals in the pursuit of acts of community (Nietzsche, 1995). No wonder *ubuntu* has been associated with virtues of respect, caring, and trust among humans (Waghid, 2014).

Secondly, from a reading of Nietzsche (1995), we infer that being and becoming human is related to the cultivation of the self in relation to other selves. And through dissent, dissonance, discord, and agreement, humans understand one another (Nietzsche, 1995). Similarly, humans bound by *ubuntu* connect with one another through iterations but also enhance their own subjective consciousness and expand their moral imaginations concerning themselves and others (Waghid, 2014, p. 68). In this way, *ubuntu* implies both looking openly and reflectively at one's own practices and, in turn, extending one's reflective openness to practices beyond one's group or community. In this sense, *ubuntu* seems highly cosmopolitan.

Thirdly, I have argued that *ubuntu* is intertwined with the notion of cosmopolitan justice (Waghid, 2014). The cultivation of cosmopolitan justice is a matter of recognising our innate humanity towards other humans, which means 'engaging them hospitably, and enacting our responsibility towards them in their difference . . . [particularly] addressing the human rights injustices people encounter on the African continent [and elsewhere]' (Waghid, 2014, p. 95). In the pursuit of cultivating cosmopolitan justice, humans should at least do three things: 'to learn to forgive; to protect those who are helpless, both morally and epistemically; and to do the unexpected, even though it goes against the grain of one's own beliefs or actions' (Waghid, 2014, p. 101).

The above understanding of *ubuntu* is constituted by both individual and collective actions. In addition, being open, reflexive, and just seems to be morally worthwhile actions that ensure the viability of any enactment of *ubuntu*. However, as an expansion of *ubuntu*, we would reckon that at least one aspect of human life seems missing. And, here, we would take us back to Nietzsche's *Human, All Too Human*, in which he makes a case close to the end of the book for the wanderer (Nietzsche, 1995, p. 302). We now want to amend the above understanding of *ubuntu* in reference to Nietzsche's idea of wandering and offer some ways to reconceptualise doctoral education.

According to Nietzsche (1995, p. 302),

> Anyone who has come even part of the way to the freedom of reason cannot feel himself to be anything other than a wanderer upon the earth – though not a traveller toward some final goal: for this does not exist. Yet he does want to observe and keep his eyes open for everything that really is going on in the world; hence, he dares not attach his heart too firmly to any individual thing; he must have something wandering within himself that finds its pleasure in change and ephemerality.

Firstly, wandering is associated with the endless pursuit of freedom of reason in everything a human does. To be concerned constantly with freedom of reason is to recognise that one's endeavours are never towards some predetermined goal but rather always linked to pursuing something new and unimaginable. In this way, there seems to be no end to one's pursuit of just human living. Secondly, a wanderer is openly aware of everything around her and does not attach herself to one particular matter for too long. To be wide awake about matters of public concern is to always work towards what is reasonable and just. Pursuing justice is endless, as moments of torture and humiliation might rise again. Thirdly, a wanderer's encounters with matters of public concern are transient so that she finds pleasure in the changes surrounding her. A wanderer devotes herself incessantly to seeing the good in the world for herself and others as she labours to suppress her inner desires that work against her aspirations for the good life. When we rethink the notion of *ubuntu* in line with wandering, humans' pursuit of cosmopolitan justice should be aligned with persistent, fleeting, and conscientious actions – nomadic or meandering actions. When humans pursue comparative education in a meandering way, they do so with resolve, transience, and attentiveness. Consequently, exercising *ubuntu* should be extended beyond notions of respect, caring, and trust among humans (Waghid, 2014) towards fleeting moments of determination and attentiveness. If humans act meanderingly there is always the possibility that they act resolutely, transiently, and attentively. Such are the virtues an extended notion of *ubuntu* brings to the discourse of comparative education. In other words, it is not enough that one exercises respect, care, and trust in dealing with comparative education. To ensure that such comparative education remains relevant and vigorous, educationists should deal with it in a resolute, transient, and attentive way as well.

Summary

In this book, I have been concerned with notions of wonder, wander, and whisper and their use in doctoral pursuits. I have argued that doctoral education, including its supervision, would be frivolous unless acted upon by wonder, wander, and whisper. To ensure the authenticity of doctoral adventures, the acts of writing and reviewing by students and supervisors should be situated in advocacy of an African philosophy of higher education and moral imagining. In turn, such an understanding of higher education ought to cultivate notions of democratic citizenship education through doctoral work that can resist hegemonic forms of authority often present in colonial, exclusionary, and unjust patterns of human subjugation.

Finally, I have argued for an expanded notion of *ubuntu* that can deal adequately with the complexities and challenges that comparative education faces. If respect for others, caring with and about them, and trusting them in communicative actions might be ways in which a comparative educational discourse can be pursued, there seem to be some virtues of human action in wandering that make humans dependent on actions of resolve, transience, and attentiveness. It might be that their actions as wanderers in the world will provoke them to act anew – that is, to act in the interest of being 'human, all too human' (Nietzsche, 1995, p. 1). My argument in defence of a cosmopolitan framework of comparative education ought to be constituted by *ubuntu* on the grounds that the latter practice invariably gives education its reflexivity, critique, and dissent associated with imaginative forms of doctoral education.

References

Agamben, G. (1999). *The man without content* (G. Albert, Trans.). Stanford University Press.
Agamben, G. (2002). *Remnants of Auschwitz: The witness and the archive* (D. Heller-Roazen, Trans.). Zone Books.
Ali, Y. (1922). *English Translation of the Propogation Centre.*
Farred, G. (Ed.). (2020). *Derrida and Africa: Jacques Derrida as a figure for African thought.* Lexington Books.
Foucault, M. (1972). *The archaeology of knowledge and the discourse on language.* Pantheon.
Gutmann, A. (2003). *Identity and democracy.* Princeton University Press.
Gyekye, K. (1997). *Tradition and modernity: Philosophical reflections on the African experience.* Oxford University Press.
Hansen, D. T. (2011). *The teacher and the world: A study of cosmopolitanism as education.* Routledge.
Martinon, J. P. (2020). Afterword: Respect for Derrida in Africa. In G. Farred (Ed.), *Derrida and Africa: Jacques Derrida as a figure for African thought* (pp. 85–93). Lexington Books.
Nietzsche, F. (1995). *Human, all too human* (G. Handwerk, Trans.). Stanford University Press.
Rancière, J. (2011). The thinking of dissensus: Politics and aesthetics. In P. Bowman & R. Stamp (Eds.), *Reading Rancière: Critical dissensus* (pp. 1–17). Continuum.
Waghid, Y. (2014). *African philosophy of education reconsidered: On being human.* Routledge.
Wiredu, K. (2000). Democracy and consensus in African traditional politics: A plea for non-party polity. In P. H. Coetzee & A. P. J. Roux (Eds.), *Philosophy from Africa: A text with readings* (pp. 374–382). Oxford University Press of Southern Africa.

Index

academic: activity 61; argumentation 30; articles 83; aspirations 19; background 83; freedom 68; responsibility 24
act(s): cosmopolitan 82; of decoloniality 7, 10, 23; of decolonisation 5, 7, 30, 45; with democratic justice 86–87; inhumane 86; of openness and reflexivity 56, 84; of provocation 22, 27, 68; of ubuntu 55, 59, 62
action(s): autonomous 60–64; deliberative 52, 62; iterative 39, 60–64; of rhythm 11
activism: intellectual 34; reflexive 65

caring 65, 90–91
citizenship 32–36

deliberation 61, 79, 85
democratic citizenship 27–30
dissensus 33, 44, 79

equal(ity) 35, 54, 58, 63, 74

freedom, academic 24, 54, 60

inclusion 10, 24, 35, 40
iteration 9, 10, 13, 39, 55–56

justice, cosmopolitan 38–40

pedagogy, critical 29, 82
philosophy of higher education 50, 54, 66, 70–76
playfulness 36
poiesis 27–31
profanation 64–68

reasonable(ness) 73, 89
reflexivity 74, 102–103, 109
rhythm(ic) 29–31, 33, 35, 43; action 20–21, 35–49

suspension 46–49

universities 18–19, 23–25, 53–54

wonder 15–19, 20–28, 42–49, 88–90
wander 62–63, 89–90, 108–109
whisper 32–37, 42–49, 88–90

Taylor & Francis eBooks

www.taylorfrancis.com

A single destination for eBooks from Taylor & Francis with increased functionality and an improved user experience to meet the needs of our customers.

90,000+ eBooks of award-winning academic content in Humanities, Social Science, Science, Technology, Engineering, and Medical written by a global network of editors and authors.

TAYLOR & FRANCIS EBOOKS OFFERS:

- A streamlined experience for our library customers
- A single point of discovery for all of our eBook content
- Improved search and discovery of content at both book and chapter level

REQUEST A FREE TRIAL
support@taylorfrancis.com

For Product Safety Concerns and Information please contact our EU representative GPSR@taylorandfrancis.com
Taylor & Francis Verlag GmbH, Kaufingerstraße 24, 80331 München, Germany

www.ingramcontent.com/pod-product-compliance
Lightning Source LLC
Chambersburg PA
CBHW071512150426
43191CB00009B/1505